CHAMPAGNE

WINE OF KINGS AND THE KING OF WINES

FOR A SPECIAL LINCOLNSHIRE LADY

Author's acknowledgements

As well as my long-suffering editor, Martin Corteel, and the rest of the crew at Carlton Books, I would like to thank the following – it wouldn't have happened without you:

Jean-Pierre Cointreau • Benoit Collard • Marinel Fitzsimons
Jean-Claude Fourmon • Martin Gamman MW • David Hesketh MW
Alastair Keeble • Alison Mann • Penelope McDonald • Freya Miller
Mel Mitchell • Lynn Murray • Frédéric Panaiotis • Françoise Peretti
Antonie Roland-Billecart • Frédéric Rouzard • Arnaud de Saignes
Patrick Schmitt MW • James Simpson MW • Jonathan Simms
Clovis Taittinger • Julia Trustram Eve

Cataloguing in Publication Data is available from the British Library

ISBN 978-1-78739-286-1

Printed in China

FSC
www.fsc.org

MIX
Paper | Supporting
responsible forestry
FSC® C104740

Headline's policy is to use papers that are natural, renewable and recyclable products and made from wood grown in well-managed forests and other controlled sources. The logging and manufacturing processes are expected to conform to the environmental regulations of the country of origin.

Editor: Martin Corteel
Design: Luke Griffin & Andri Johannsson
Picture Research: Paul Langan
Production: Rachel Burgess

HEADLINE PUBLISHING GROUP LIMITED
An Hachette UK Company
Carmelite House
50 Victoria Embankment
London EC4Y 0DZ

The authorised representative in the EEA is Hachette Ireland,
8 Castlecourt Centre, Dublin 15, D15 XTP3, Ireland (email: info@hbgi.ie)

www.headline.co.uk
www.hachette.co.uk

OPPOSITE Chardonnay growing in the fine belemnite chalk soils of Le Mesnil-sur-Oger, a grand cru village in the Côte des Blancs. As well as being a superb reservoir of water and source of reflected heat, chalk adds a mineral precision to champagne.

PAGE SIX Gleaming bottles of Champagne Cattier on display in the cellars of this bespoke family-owned house in Chigny-les-Roses, a flower-bedecked village in the Montagne de Reims.

CHAMPAGNE

WINE OF KINGS AND THE KING OF WINES

TOM BRUCE-GARDYNE

WELBECK

CONTENTS

INTRODUCTION

"THINK PLEASURE, THINK PARTIES, THINK CELEBRATION … THINK CHAMPAGNE" HAS BEEN THE MANTRA OF THIS MOST BEGUILING DRINK FOR CENTURIES. WE CAN ALL PICTURE AN ICE-COLD BOTTLE PLUCKED FROM THE FRIDGE, THE FOIL RIPPED OFF AND THE WIRE CAGE REMOVED. A BRIEF PAUSE OF ANTICIPATION AS THE CORK SLOWLY EMERGES, AND THEN THAT JOYOUS "POP" – SIGNALLING THE PARTY HAS TRULY BEGUN.

The release of pressure unlocks the energy in the bottle, creating around a million bubbles in each glass according to scientific research. What the science explains as well is that the escaping CO_2 tickles not just our tongue but also a valve in our tummy, propelling the alcohol into the bloodstream and up to the brain. To achieve the same buzz with still wine takes that much longer, or a serious workout on the dance floor. With champagne the bubbles do the dancing for you.

Other sparkling wines will give you the same effect, but there is something special about champagne. It is a word loaded with symbolism around sensuality, glamour and decadence. Champagne needs to be a luxury, or else it loses meaning. When Woolworth's sold it for £5 under its "Worth It!" label in a publicity stunt in 2007, anyone given a bottle might have adapted that hoary old catchphrase of L'Oréal and decided "it's because I'm not worth it". Yet, of course, plenty of champagne brands know how to exploit the idea of being "reassuringly expensive" and part of that celebrity lifestyle to which we allegedly aspire.

But cut through the marketing froth, and there's a fascinating story to champagne, not least how those bubbles got there in the first place. To set the scene, *Champagne: Wine of Kings and the King of Wines* begins with the winemaking process and a brief history. For many years it was a complete mystery how and why champagne sparkled in this relatively cool corner of north-east France on the edge of planet wine. Was it something in the earth or in the stars? Or was it some ancient curse that caused endless bottles to shatter under the pressure? Eventually the Champenoise came to realise those fiendish bubbles were their greatest asset.

The modern era saw the rise of the great Champagne Houses, and their individual stories are continued in the middle part of the book. Beyond the big, familiar names lie some huge co-operatives that now have sizeable brands of their own. And behind them are the thousands of growers who tend the vines and perhaps dream of making their own wine. Those with land in the right place and sufficient self-belief and passion are doing just that with a myriad of grower champagnes that really do express the *terroir* of their vineyards.

Next there's an exploration of some of the myriad sparkling wines that champagne has inspired, from New Zealand to California's Napa Valley. There has been the phenomenal success of Italian prosecco and the rise of English sparkling wine that may one day become champagne's most serious rival. The final part of the book looks at the culture of champagne and how it has been refracted through the lens of cinema, art and literature. Throughout *Champagne: Wine of Kings and the King of Wines* the aim is to celebrate this extraordinary wine in images as much as words, plundering the region's rich archive to bring the story alive.

Tom Bruce-Gardyne
2019

PART 1

THE ESSENTIALS OF CHAMPAGNE

THE VINEYARDS OF CHAMPAGNE AND THE DECISION TO FOCUS ON THREE GRAPE VARIETIES HAS BEEN A SLOW EVOLUTION OVER CENTURIES, AS HAS THE WINEMAKING PROCESS. TODAY IT IS THE MOST VALUABLE AND WELL-PROTECTED WINE REGION IN THE WORLD, WHILE THE PREDOMINANT STYLE OF CHAMPAGNE HAS SHIFTED FROM A LATE VICTORIAN SWEETNESS TO BONE DRY.

PREVIOUS PAGES A new dawn as the sun rises over the vineyards of the Montagne de Reims.

OPPOSITE Healthy bunches of freshly picked chardonnay and pinot noir – two of the three classic champagne grapes. Champagne is almost invariably a blend unless a pure chardonnay Blanc de Blancs is used.

THE CHAMPAGNE REGION

TO THE ENGLISH THE UNDULATING SLOPES AND FAMOUS CHALKY SOILS OF THE CHAMPAGNE REGION ARE REMINISCENT OF THE SOUTH DOWNS OF SUSSEX AND KENT. FROM A GEOLOGICAL POINT OF VIEW THIS MAKES PERFECT SENSE BECAUSE THE DOWNS ARE A CONTINUATION OF CHAMPAGNE, SEPARATED ONLY BY THE CHANNEL.

The Romans christened the region Campania, after the southern Italian province, and the name evolved into Champagne. The region starts in the Marne valley, just 35 miles east of Paris, and extends north of Reims and as far south as the outlying district of the Aube, just beyond the northern tip of Burgundy. Within this wide perimeter that covers five *départements* – Marne, Aisne, Aube, Haute-Marne and Seine-en-Marne – are 319 villages blessed with the right to produce champagne.

Around these villages the countryside can appear a complete monoculture with nothing but row upon row of manicured vines angled to catch the maximum sunlight. They are subdivided into neat parcels such that every available scrap of land in the *appellation's* 34,500 hectares is planted. In between the villages, however, are large forests and swathes of farmland whose crops can only look on with envy at the carefully tended and immensely profitable vineyards of Champagne.

That the word 'champagne' should be considered a unique geographic region and not just a particular style of sparkling wine

has been crucial to the wine's success. Had the Champenois failed to map out the *appellation* and then defend it vigorously around the world, this quintessential luxury fizz would have become as generic as Yorkshire pudding. As a number of the big Champagne Houses have proved, you can produce a fine imitation elsewhere using the same process and the exact same grapes. But if you want to make champagne you can do so only in the eponymous region. That is what the French have long maintained, and today just about everyone agrees with them. The only exceptions are a few, die-hard Americans who continue to produce domestic 'champagne' for the US market only.

Within the Champagne region are five key areas, which, running north to south, start with:

THE MONTAGNE DE REIMS
Maybe the French were being *ironique*, but you don't need crampons or oxygen to reach the 275m summit of this upland

BELOW The fizziest town in France and probably the world, Épernay is the epicentre of Champagne. It sits above an endless network of chalk cellars, where millions of bottles lie ageing in the dark.

plateau between Reims and Épernay which is capped with a thickly wooded national park. The region is famed for its pinot noir that accounts for 40% of plantings compared to 36% for pinot meunier and 24% for chardonnay. Beneath the trees, the northern slopes are carpeted with vines all the way round to the Grand Cru villages of Verzenay, Verzy and Sillery to the north-east. While to the south are the villages of Ambonnay, Louvois and Bouzy, also Grand Cru, which produce a slightly richer version of pinot noir than the firmer, more angular styles to the north.

CÔTE DES BLANCS

As the name suggests, the region's white grape, chardonnay, dominates: four-fifths of these slopes south of Épernay are planted with it. Towards the top of the steepest vineyards in the Grand Cru village of Cramant, the chalk breaks through the topsoil to help produce wines of a searing, bone-dry, mineral intensity that can sometimes age for decades. Cramant's neighbours to the south – Avize, Oger and Le Mesnil-sur-Oger – and Chouilly to the north, are also all Grand Cru. While the Premier Cru village of Vertus, at the

BELOW Detailed maps of the Champagne region, the upper one focusing on the villages, vineyards and Champagne Houses of the Montagne de Reims and Éperon de Bouzy and the lower one on \the Vallée de la Marne.

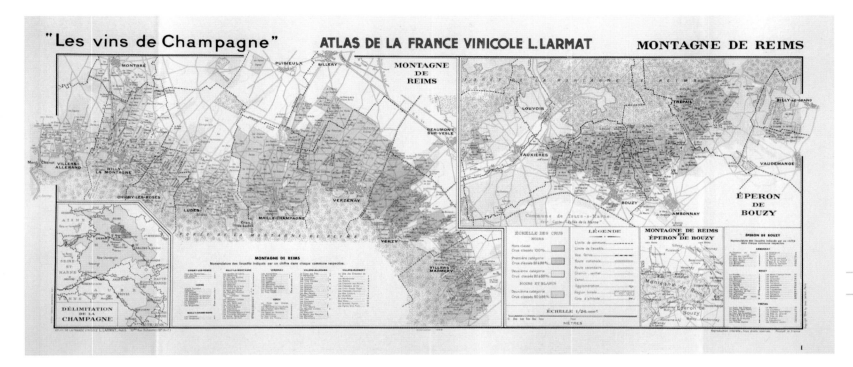

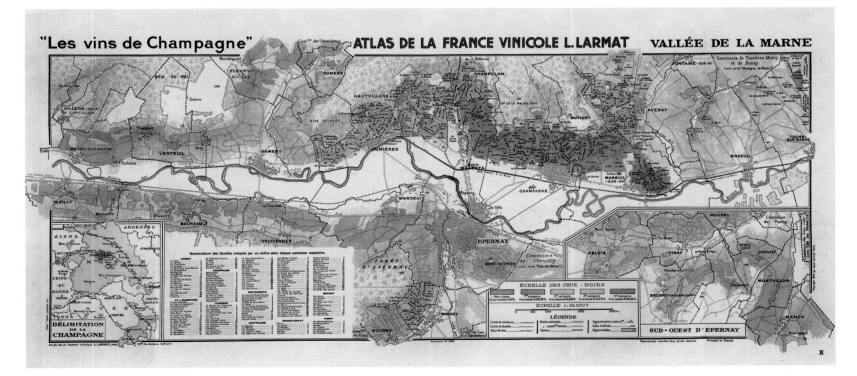

southern end of the Côte des Blancs, represents a lone outpost of fine pinot noir.

VALLÉE DE LA MARNE

The third key area stretches downstream along the Marne, producing wines once known as *vins de la rivière*. It begins with Aÿ, just east of Épernay, which vies with Sillery as the most historic name in the whole of Champagne. In the fifteenth century, Francis I declared he was king of Aÿ, and not just king of France, while Pope Leo the Magnificent would drink little else but the wines from this famous village. With its majestic Grand Cru vineyards sloping down to the Marne, Aÿ is home to some of the greatest pinot noir in the region and such esteemed Houses as Ayala, Bollinger and Deutz.

Around Épernay are Dizzy, Hautvilliers and Cumières, before you progress along the valley to the village of Château-Thierry and the western edges of Champagne. The chalk, so close to the topsoil around Aÿ, slips deeper underground as you move west, and the quality also decreases slightly, particularly on the north-facing slopes of the left bank. Some excellent pinot meunier is produced nonetheless, and this grape accounts for almost two-thirds of plantings in the Vallée de la Marne.

ABOVE These painted, half-timbered houses, dating from the sixteenth century, are a feature of the ancient town of Troyes that, unlike Reims, survived the First World War intact. It is the capital of the Aube, or Côte des Bars as it's known in champagne circles.

CÔTE DE SÉZANNE AND THE CÔTE DES BAR

The Côte de Sézanne is really a continuation of the Côte des Blancs, separated by the Saint Gond marshes, and with a similar preference for chardonnay, which makes up two-thirds of plantings. The wines are not as prestigious, however, and most find their way into NV blends. Much larger in area is the Aube, or Côte des Bar as it is now called, which was once given over to gamay, and is now almost 90% pinot noir. With so little to spare from the Montaigne de Reims, particularly the Grand Cru and Premier Cru vineyards, this is *the* place every well-known Champagne House comes to source its pinot noir. As well as some of the prettiest countryside in Champagne, the Aube also boasts one of the hottest new areas for top-quality chardonnay planted on pure chalk on the slopes of the Montgueux hill, west of Troyes.

ABOVE The *grand cru* village of Cramant in the Côte des Blancs with its immaculate vineyards of chardonnay stretching out in front.

RIGHT A detailed map of the famous villages of the Côte des Blancs and its mix of Grand Crus and Premier Crus vineyards.

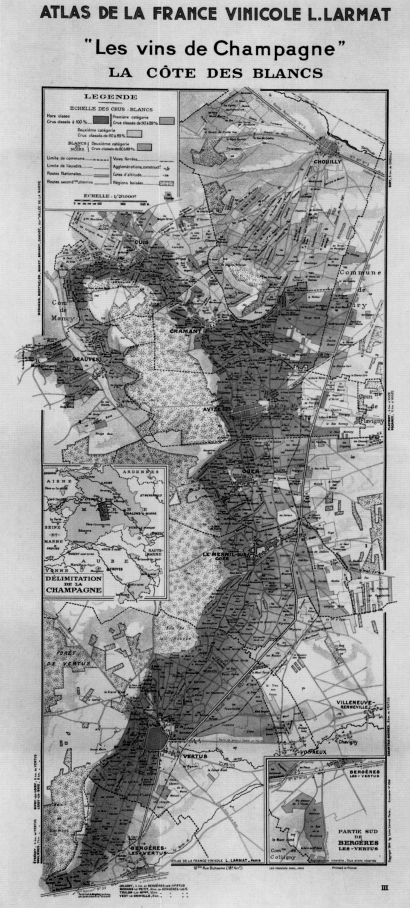

TERROIR

IT IS A GOOD TWO-HOUR DRIVE TO CROSS THE CHAMPAGNE REGION FROM WEST TO EAST OR
NORTH TO SOUTH, WHICH ALLOWS FOR PLENTY OF VARIATION IN ALL THE FACTORS THAT MAKE
UP THAT GLORIOUSLY FRENCH, CATCH-ALL WORD *TERROIR*. THE WORD EVOKES SUCH NATURAL,
GOD-GIVEN VARIABLES AS RAINFALL, ELEVATION, SOIL AND SUNLIGHT.

As in other wine regions, the best vineyards are on the slopes, usually halfway up and facing east or south-east to soak up as much early-morning sunshine as possible. There is a maritime influence in the heart of Champagne around Reims and Épernay and this helps to moderate the climate. That influence fades as you head south towards the Aube, where the climate has a more continental feel.

And yet there is no escaping the human factor in all this. In the vineyard the grower will decide which clone of which grape to plant and on which rootstock. He or she will also determine the density of vines per hectare, what training system to use, how to prune, what to spray and, crucially, when to harvest. In the cellar the balance tips firmly away from nature in favour of man. In his *World Encyclopedia of Champagne & Sparkling Wine*, Tom Stevenson compares champagne with port and sherry, and writes: "It is impossible to produce such wines with a hands-off approach.

They are the result of human meddling, intervention and sophistication and, of all these wines, champagne is perhaps the most technical, most demanding and most man-made." The ethos of the Champagne Houses, especially for their flagship, non-vintage expressions, is to produce something that never varies from one year to the next.

The vagaries of climate and, to some extent the essence of *terroir* itself, are blended away with grapes sourced from all four corners of Champagne and by using reserve wines from previous vintages to create a consistent house style. Like the big brand-owners of Scotch whisky, the secret is all in the blend. The component parts, whether from a particular distillery or vineyard, are like instruments in an orchestra whereby the whole is greater than the sum of its parts, or so people claim. But as in Scotland, this theory is being challenged. Today there are a swathe of expensive, single-vineyard champagnes like Krug's

BELOW The steep, south-facing slopes of Philipponnat's fabled Clos des Goisses vineyards in Mareuil-sur-Aÿ. The water, a canal beside the River Marne, helps stabilise the climate.

Clos du Mesnil and Philipponnat's pioneering Clos des Goisses that first appeared in 1935. There are also many more grower champagnes keen to express the uniqueness of their vineyards, as a point of difference to the *négociants'* blends.

Champagne's original '*terroir-ist*' was René Lamarre, author of *La Révolution champenoise*. In the late nineteenth century he railed against the brand-owners as explained in the following passage from Kolleen Guy's fascinating book, *When Champagne Became French*: "By monopolizing production and promoting brand names through the Syndicat du Commerce, Lamarre argued, the négociants severed the wine from the heart and soul of Champagne, unjustly accruing all of the regional riches in the process. Terroir was being sacrificed to greed."

Zoom out of Champagne and you will discover it straddles latitude 49° north, the same as Quebec and Vancouver. This is on the cusp of where you can make wine in the northern hemisphere, and occasionally beyond – as it was during the mini ice age in the late seventeenth century. Today this limit is being edged northwards with annual temperatures rising by 1°C over the last 30–50 years. What really matters is the temperature during the growing season, which currently ranges from 14.7°C–16.1°C. In a good year the vines will have escaped any risk of a late frost to ripen gradually after flowering, ideally for 100 days before the harvest. The aim is to pick grapes that are fully mature yet retain the acidity vital for any quality sparkling wine.

That 100-day period is significantly shortened in scorching hot summers like that of 2003. Average growing season temperatures are predicted to rise by 0.4°C in the next decade, which sounds promising for producers in Sussex, but less so for those in Champagne. Then again, it's a bit more complicated than that because southern England has a far more maritime climate. Besides, there is plenty producers can do – in the vineyard with canopy management of the leaves, and in the cellar, by altering the *dosage* – to dampen the impact of climate change.

CHALK

It is hard to exaggerate the importance of chalky soils in Champagne. Being so porous, chalk acts as a superb subterranean reservoir for the vines, holding up to 400 litres of water per cubic metre, while offering good drainage so the roots don't become waterlogged. It also acts as a solar panel to reflect sunlight and warmth on to the vine, and it adds a mineral precision to the wines, particularly chardonnay. In addition, its relative abundance attracted the Romans to mine the stuff and produce quicklime and whitewash for their buildings. By extending the mineshafts, the Champenois created the labyrinthine network of tunnels, or *crayères*, which have proved the perfect environment for a slow secondary fermentation in the bottle.

Of the various strains of chalk, the best is said to be belemnite from the remains of extinct sea creatures; this whole region was beneath the ocean until some 70 million years ago. The strata of chalk were pushed up by subsequent volcanic activity, and occasionally break through the surface. These chalky outcrops are known as the *Falaises de Champagne* and are most evident in prime sites on the Côte des Blancs and Montaigne de Reims. There are less porous types of chalk and a whole range of other soils including clay, marl, limestone and sandstone. Marl, for example, is richer in nutrients but doesn't drain so well, which can lead to fungal diseases in damp years.

TOP Part of Champagne Taittinger's 250-hectare estate; note how the rows of vines are angled to make best use of the sun's rays.

ABOVE Pure belemnite chalk in the Côte des Blancs, which lends great mineral precision to the chardonnay grown here.

THE CHAMPAGNE GRAPES

HAVING SET THE SCENE, IT IS TIME TO INTRODUCE THE CAST. OVER THE CENTURIES THE NUMBER OF GRAPE VARIETIES IN CHAMPAGNE HAVE BEEN WHITTLED DOWN TO JUST THREE, WITH THE LAST MAIN CONTENDER, GAMAY, BANISHED FROM THE AUBE IN THE 1960s. THE THREE ARE: PINOT NOIR, CHARDONNAY AND PINOT MEUNIER.

However, the choice of what variety to plant in which vineyard is greater than you might think if you consider there are more than 50 approved clones available, each with subtly different attributes. Pinot noir and chardonnay are the classic grapes of Burgundy, and it took a fair few centuries for the region's producers to finally concede they would never beat their southern neighbours when it came to still wines. Today, almost the sole survivors in Champagne of this ancient tradition of still wines are both made of pinot noir. From near Épernay, there is a tiny production of the delightfully named Bouzy Rouge from the eponymous village, pronounced 'boozy'. While from the Aube you can find the pink Rosé des Riceys.

As for the whites, one imagines the Burgundians were never remotely fazed by the still chardonnays once produced in Champagne. Here, in its raw state as *vin clair*, it seems skeletal with almost no flesh at all, and appears to contain enough acid to strip the enamel from your teeth. In this chilly, marginal climate, this is a variety that craves that little extra boost of alcohol and the gush of bubbles from a secondary fermentation. Within Champagne, 28.5% of the vineyards are planted with chardonnay. It is held in high esteem for its crisp elegance and finesse, particularly in its heartland of the Côte des Blancs. For blends it adds a racy backbone and freshness, while on its own as a Blanc de Blancs it can outlive any other style of champagne thanks to its acidity. With the very finest vintage *cuvées*, this recedes after a decade or two to reveal a toasty, almost Burgundian richness. Needless to say, even those who profess to hate chardonnay, guzzle it with glee.

By a small margin, pinot noir is the most planted grape in Champagne, accounting for 38.4% of the vineyards. The core area is the Montaigne de Reims, though it doesn't dominate to the same extent as chardonnay on the Côte des Blancs. It also soaks up the sunshine on the south-facing slopes of the right bank of the Marne, and accounts for four-fifths of plantings in the Côte des Bars – the prime source of pinot noir for standard non-vintage blends. Since the days of Dom Pérignon, this grape has been very gently crushed

BELOW LEFT Chardonnay lends elegance and a racy acidity to all champagne blends that are not classified – Blanc de Noirs, and stars in its own solo performance as Blanc de Blancs.

BELOW The other Burgundy grape – pinot noir, is the most planted variety in Champagne, accounting for just under 40% of the vines. It is also used to produce the region's still red wine – Bouzy Rouge.

to avoid the clear-run juice being tinted by the skins.

Marginally less 'noble' is the third grape, pinot meunier, which covers 32.8% of Champagne's vineyards at present. Being a relatively late-budding variety, and thus less prone to late frosts, it is widely planted on the cooler, north-facing slopes of the Marne valley. Here it has been losing ground to pinot noir, with its vineyards down 7% since the 1980s according to the champagne expert, Michael Edwards. "This appears, at least in some cases, to have been driven by fashion and marketing, rather than by any serious concern to improve quality," he wrote in *The Finest Wines of Champagne*.

The vineyards are densely planted with 8–10,000 vines per hectare to ensure a healthy competition between them as their roots stretch out in search of water and nutrients from the soil. A month after the harvest, once the weather has turned cold, growers descend on their vineyards armed with pruning shears. The idea is to encourage each vine to concentrate its energies on a selected number of fruit-bearing buds and to stop them becoming too leafy. Proud of their pruning prowess, the growers aim to achieve the right balance of foliage to bunches of grapes, of which there should be 12–15, enough to produce one bottle per vine.

Under the rules of champagne, the grapes are all picked by hand because machine harvesting might damage the bunches and risk skin contact with the juice. The grapes are then quickly crushed as whole bunches, and separated into the *cuvée*, with the first three gentle presses, and the *tailles*, or tails, which are squeezed that much harder. In a bid to improve quality the Comité Interprofessionnel du vin de Champagne (CIVC) reduced the amount producers could extract from the *taille* by around a fifth in 1992.

Each pressing is kept separate to allow the winemaker more scope in constructing the particular blend. Multiply the number of pressings from a single plot by the number of vineyards, the range of grapes and different vintages, and you have an almost infinite spectrum of base wines to choose from. That said, the difference between these component parts tends to be very subtle since the base wine is, almost by definition, relatively neutral, low in alcohol and high in acidity.

From whatever cards nature has dealt, the winemaker, or *chef de cave*, has to try and shuffle them into a consistent house style, with a little help from the reserve wines of former years, unless making vintage champagne. This is no mean feat given the vagaries of the weather up here on the northern fringes of planet wine. Yet for the real artist in the cellar the cult of consistency must grate at times. Occasionally he or she will be invited to unleash their creative genius and construct something new, but it doesn't happen very often.

LEFT The long, painstaking job of pruning the vines lasts from November through to March and sometimes April.

BELOW The other component in the champagne mix is pinot meunier, these having just been picked in the Marne Valley, where it dominates the north-facing slopes.

HOW CHAMPAGNE IS MADE

THE BUBBLES THAT DEFINE CHAMPAGNE HAVE BEEN PART OF WINEMAKING FOR EVER. THEY SIGNIFY THE START OF FERMENTATION AFTER THE GRAPES HAVE BEEN CRUSHED AND THE END WHEN THE BUBBLING STOPS.

For the earliest winemakers this was the only visible sign that anything was actually happening. They couldn't see the few billion wild yeast cells attack the grape juice in a feeding frenzy until all the sugars had been converted to alcohol. What they were witnessing was the by-product of fermentation – carbon dioxide, which, if trapped in the bottle, will make any wine sparkle.

The story of sparkling wine has been a long slow evolution from accident to design. In an area like Champagne on the northern fringes of the wine world, it was always a challenge to complete fermentation before the cold weather put the yeast to sleep for the winter. Come the spring, the warm weather would rekindle the process causing the wine to fizz in cask or bottle. Local winemakers long considered this to be a curse until ironically it became the region's greatest virtue.

Secondary fermentation in bottle evolved into a precise science and today the process is as follows: the champagne grapes of chardonnay, pinot noir and pinot meunier are harvested by hand and quickly pressed at the winery to separate the juice from the skins. Around four-fifths will be the *cuvée*, until the pressure in the presses is increased to extract the final *taille*, or tail. This might be sold off or blended back in to add structure to the wine.

The Champagne Houses buy in grapes from across the region and ferment them separately, as they do with the different grape varieties. Fermentation takes place in stainless-steel tanks, and sometimes in new or old oak barrels. Once complete, the cellars will be full of separate tanks of fairly neutral, acidic base wine with a strength of around 11.5%. There will be subtle differences between them, however, and this gives the winemaker the means

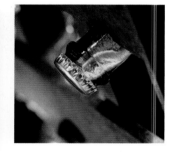

ABOVE Most champagne is aged with a beer-like crown cap before *dégorgement* when the sediment is removed and the bottle is stoppered with a champagne cork.

FAR LEFT Freshly picked chardonnay in a traditional 'Coquard' press found in many Champagne Houses. The key is to press the grapes as quickly as possible before the juice begins to oxidise.

LEFT The time-honoured practice of riddling bottles in *pupitres* in the cellar. The technique, invented by Veuve Clicquot's *chef de cave* in the early nineteenth century, aims to jiggle the yeasty sediment into the neck of the bottle.

to construct the house style. The blend, or *assemblage*, is created from January to March and involves blending in reserve wines from previous years in the case of non-vintage champagnes, which account for the vast majority of bottles drunk. They are easy to spot with their 'NV' on the label.

Vintage champagne with 100% of the grapes from a specific year, or a *cru* from a particular vineyard, will seek to express the vagaries of climate or *terroir*, while the dominant NV style is all about consistency. Either way, constructing the blend is almost certainly the most skilful part of the whole process. Once finished, the wine will be racked into a clean tank and injected with the *liqueur de tirage* – a mix of sugar, champagne yeasts and some nutrients before bottling under a crown cap, like a beer bottle. The amount of sugar and yeast is carefully calibrated to achieve a precise pressure of up to 7 bar, akin to the tyre pressure of a double-decker bus.

The bottles are stacked horizontally in the cold, dank cellars of Champagne, and left to get on with it. The cellars form mile upon mile of tunnels hacked into the soft chalk, deep underground where the temperature remains a constant 10–12°C throughout the year. The yeasts have been specially cultured to cope with the chill and work under pressure as they feed on the sugar to boost the strength by a degree and create all those wonderful bubbles. The process can take up to three months, until all the yeast cells expire and sink to the bottom as lees. It is assumed they die happy, but their role is not over.

All champagne must be bottle-aged for a minimum of 15 months, of which at least a year will be on the lees. The dead cells start to break down in a slow process known as autolysis, which can last up to three or four years in the case of a prestigious vintage *cuvée*. Most champagnes are not given time for the full effects to appear, but this is where those subtle, nutty, toasty, brioche-like aromas come from.

The need to get shot of the lees in the bottle without losing the fizz was a conundrum the Champenois finally solved, through a process known as *remuage*. Traditionally this was done with a *pupitre*, which resembles a hefty, wooden sandwich board drilled with champagne-sized holes. Bottles were inserted at 45 degrees and gradually tilted each day with a vigorous shake of the wrist until all the yeasty sediment was down in the neck of the bottle. This riddling of the bottles by hand takes four to five weeks. As well as being extremely labour-intensive it probably caused a certain amount of repetitive strain injury. If you visit a Champagne House, or any producer of traditional sparkling wine, you will see rows of *pupitres* proudly displayed in the cellars. Behind the scenes, a rather more hi-tech if less glamorous solution has been found – the *gyropallette*, where a computerised machine can riddle a whole pallet of bottles in three to four days.

The next step is *dégorgement* where the neck of the upturned bottle is frozen, usually in liquid nitrogen, and the crown cap removed. The icy plug of yeast, about an inch long, shoots out like a champagne cork thanks to the pressure. The bottle is immediately topped up with a mix of the same wine and sugar syrup known as the *liqueur d'expédition* and corked before too many bubbles escape.

TOP Most champagne producers now use stainless steel tanks for fermentation rather than traditional oak barrels. This ensures that no extraneous aromatic components get conveyed and allows for a more pure wine.

ABOVE The final stage in the process before the bottle is corked is adding the *liqueur d'expédition* – a mix of wine and a carefully calibrated quantity of sugar to determine the *dosage*.

VINTAGES AND STYLES

THE LAST ACT OF MANIPULATION BEFORE THE CORK IS RAMMED HOME, IS THE *DOSAGE* – OR QUANTITY OF SUGAR CONTAINED WITHIN THE *LIQUEUR D'EXPÉDITION*. THE SUGAR LEVEL STARTS FROM LESS THAN 2G/LITRE OF SUGAR AND GOES UP TO MORE THAN 50G/L.

For those who like their fizz drier than the driest Martini with no added sugar, there is *Brut Nature* – also known as *Non-Dosé*, *Ultra Brut*, *Brut Sauvage* or, for the skinniest supermodel, *Brut Zéro*. Technically it can have up to 2g/litre of sugar, not that you would notice. It became trendy in the 1980s with the launch of Laurent-Perrier's *Ultra Brut*, which inspired other houses to follow suit. While the style excited a number of sommeliers, sales were tiny. The trend seems to be fading now, not least because the wines often tasted hollow and unbalanced.

Next up is the merely searingly dry *Extra Brut* where up to 6g/litre of sugar are allowed. If the wine is really well made, such a low *dosage* can work. Then comes *Brut*, where the maximum sugar content is increased to 12g/litre. Given that the word translates as 'raw', and that it was off the scale of dryness for most champagne drinkers a century ago, certainly outside London, it has come

a long way. Today even those sweet-toothed Russians have succumbed to the raw charms of *Brut*, which today accounts for well over 90% of all champagne sold.

Beyond 12 grams you get to *Extra-Sec* or *Extra-Dry*. It has all but disappeared thanks to the global domination of *Brut* and a certain snobbish contempt for anything not bone-dry. Above 17 grams you are in the territory of *Sec* or 'Dry', before you hit *Demi-Sec* (33–50g/l) and finally *Doux* at over 50g/l. The terminology appears terribly dated since so-called 'dry champagne' would definitely be sweet by today's standards.

The evolution of sweetness is evident from Louis Roederer's Carte Blanche that boasted a sumptuous 180g/l of sugar in the early twentieth century. By the 1980s that had been cut by two-thirds, and today the wine contains 45g/l, putting it on the sweet side of *Demi-Sec*. Meanwhile within *Brut* there has been a shift

LEFT While there are myriad different brands of champagne, one style has come to dominate – non-vintage (NV) Brut with a *dosage* typically around 9–12g/litre of sugar. Today it accounts for a good 80% of sales.

to drier styles according to the *Drinks Business* editor Patrick Schmitt. When he researched the subject for his Master of Wine dissertation, he discovered that average *dosage* levels had fallen by 25% in the last 20 years, with most producers citing the 2003 heat wave as the turning point. So is it all due to climate change?

Not according to Schmitt, who believes the main reason is down to the winemakers pursuing a drier style, which they prefer and believe their customers do too. Apparently this is backed up by a detailed study carried out by Moët & Chandon a few years ago. Whether consumer tastes have really become drier is a moot point, especially when you consider the success of Extra-Dry Prosecco.

More than 80% of champagne is **non-vintage** and designated NV on the label. The amount of previous vintages included in the blend varies depending on the house style. A fresh, lively wine like Taittinger NV might contain barely one-tenth of a previous year, while something with the richness of Krug can stretch back over multiple vintages, with only half coming from the most recent one. Other NV champagnes might be entirely from a single year. They are not designed to improve with age on release, but that's not to say they won't if the quality is there and provided the bottles are stored somewhere cool and dark at a reasonably constant temperature of 10–15°C. Beyond a year or two, any improvements will be negligible until eventually the freshness starts to fade.

Vintage champagne does improve over time, especially if its producer gave it a good three or four years resting on its lees in the cellar before being disgorged. If you love those toasty, biscuit-like aromas and flavours of fine vintage fizz, you should resist drinking the wine until a decade or so after the harvest. Such bottles imply the growing season was especially good, although not all producers are as discerning as others, and some will release a vintage almost every year.

The category has come under pressure from the top layer of champagnes, known as **prestige cuvées**. Sourcing the greatest vintages from the best vineyards available, the *chef de cave* of every Grand Marque will endeavour to blend the finest expression possible. The target audience demands nothing less and has the means to pay – although the market has shifted somewhat from those Russian Czars sipping Louis Roederer in lead crystal bottles at the Imperial Court. While some houses focus all the high-end efforts on prestige *cuvées*, those that have persisted with vintage champagne are beginning to look relatively good value.

Champagne is invariably a blend of grapes, unless it is a pure chardonnay **Blanc de Blancs**. With its crisp, whip-clean effervescence and lemony freshness, this is often the lightest and most elegant style. By contrast, **Blanc de Noirs**, made from just black grapes, usually have a riper texture, with aromas of baked apple and spice, for example. You might find a deeper, more golden hue in a Blanc de Noirs, but no tinge of pink. For that there is **rosé champagne**, which is usually made from blending in a little red wine. All still rosé in Europe, from Puglia to Provence, is made by letting the colour from the skins bleed into the juice before it is run off. Simply marrying red and white wine is what the Californians do to make their sweet, bubblegum-pink blush wine, yet it seems to work in Champagne, often beautifully. And, though some Champenois prefer the skin contact method, it can be difficult to control the tannins.

LEFT Led by houses like Pommery, the first Brut champagnes began to gain popularity in England in the 1870s. Some went further, like Laurent-Perrier *sans-sucre* or *Zéro Dosage* wine, released a decade later.

BELOW Rosé once dismissed by many in the industry as being not altogether serious, has become one of the most exciting and dynamic categories of champagne.

SERVING, STORING AND BIBLICAL BOTTLES

ONCE UPON A TIME GOING DOWN TO THE CELLAR TO FETCH A BOTTLE OF CHAMPAGNE WAS A GAME OF RUSSIAN ROULETTE. THE SLIGHTEST FLAW IN THE GLASS COULD TURN ANY BOTTLE INTO A LETHAL WEAPON.

One can imagine his Lordship in his drawing room startled by a muffled commotion from the bowels of his house, followed by the deep groan of an injured butler. Mercifully such accidents were abolished with the invention of strong, flawless glass in the nineteenth century.

Stronger bottles encouraged producers to ramp up the pressure to between 5 and 6 atmospheres at room temperature. If you were foolish enough to open champagne that warm, the cork would shoot out like a bullet, foam would spurt everywhere and what was left of the wine would go flat dely fast. Unless you are a Formula One racing driver intent on spraying the crowds from the podium, this is best avoided.

However if the bottle is chilled down to 5°C, the pressure drops to 2.5 atmospheres, though you should still take care to point it away from anyone and hold your thumb over the cork as you free it from its wire cage. Then twist the bottle and let the cork ease itself out with no gush of foam. It sounds obvious, but accidents do happen. As retold in Don Hewitson's *Glory of Champagne* "*The Evening Standard* reported a doctor from Moorfield Eye Hospital saying: 'We get at least two victims of champagne corks a week and often have to operate.'" Today it might well be a Prosecco cork.

Alternatively, you may wish to unleash your inner Cossack, and slice open the bottle with a sabre. The rules of *sabrage*, as it is known, are as follows: make sure the bottle is well chilled and dry so it doesn't slip, and then take off the wire, strip off the foil and hold the bottle by the base, angled upwards. Make sure your thumb is tucked out of harm's way inside the punt, and that no one is in your line of fire. Then run the blade up the seam in the glass along the side of the bottle in a firm, gentle sweep. As you hit the glass collar on the neck it will fly off with a crack, taking the cork with it. Thanks to all that pressure in the bottle, it is easier than it looks.

And you don't need a sabre – a big kitchen knife works just as well.

Champagne should be served at a chilly 5–9°C because it will warm up in the glass, but over-chilling a bottle, as can happen with ice buckets in a restaurant, will blunt the aromas and flavours. As for the glass, fashions have swung from the *coupe* to the flute to the tulip-shaped wine glass. The *coupe*, or saucer, is the oldest, in fact even older than its supposed inspiration – Marie Antoinette's left breast. There are tales of how the teenage queen would dress up as a milkmaid at her summer palace of Rambouillet, and that the king commissioned a *bol sein*, or breast bowl, for her dairy.

In truth the champagne coupe was an Anglo-Italian invention of the 1660s from Venetian glassblowers employed by the Duke of Buckingham in London. Yet it was too good a myth to die, and recently supermodels Claudia Schiffer and Kate Moss have both bared their breasts for a modern version.

A pyramid of champagne saucers filled with fizz has a certain cheesy glamour, and the world record set in 2008 in a Dutch shopping mall contained some 40,000 glasses, 63 storeys high. Yet the *coupe* has been banished to the cocktail bar thanks to its Babycham image and because the *mousse* of bubbles that took so long to create dissipate far

FAR LEFT If you are tempted to unleash your inner Cossack and perform *sabrage* on a bottle of champagne, make sure your thumb is safely tucked into the punt.

LEFT In 2014 Kate Moss became the latest celebrity to have a champagne coup modelled on one of her breasts, following the almost certainly mythical story about Marie Antoinette.

BIBLICAL BOTTLES

Champagne comes in many sizes, from those often disappointing quarter-sized 'piccolo' bottles served on airlines, to those of truly biblical proportions.

MAGNUM
Two bottles (1.5l). Latin for 'great', and considered ideal for ageing vintage champagne.

JEROBOAM
Four bottles (3l). Named after the tenth-century king of northern Israel, and meaning 'he increases the people'.

REHOBOAM
Six bottles (4.5l). The son of Solomon, whose name means 'he who enlarges the people'.

METHUSELAH
Eight bottles (6l). Symbolic of great age, and named after an Old Testament patriarch who lived for 969 years.

SALMANAZAR
12 bottles (9l). Named after the Assyrian king Shalmaneser.

BALTHAZAR
16 bottles (12l). Named after the king of Arabia who presented gifts to the baby Jesus.

NEBUCHADNEZZAR
20 bottles (15l). Named after the most powerful of all Babylonian kings, who ruled from the late seventh to the middle sixth century BC.

Beyond lies the Solomon at 24 bottles and the Sovereign at 35 bottles, according to Taittinger, possibly the only producer. For one bottle more there is the Primat, and finally the Melchizedek, or Midas, which boasts the equivalent of 40 bottles. As of 2016, one sprayed in gold metallic paint from Armand de Brignac (Ace of Spades), would cost you £39,995 with free postage, but no guarantee it will fit in the average fridge.

too quickly. Champagne flutes are a lot better, though they are often too small and overfilled so you cannot properly appreciate the wine's aromas. As a result a standard, tulip-shaped white wine glass is now favoured. Then again, you will get through more bottles than with flutes, which might be a consideration if you are paying for the party. And as for missing out on the bouquet you wonder how many guests would actually notice. Personally I have never seen anyone swirl and sniff a glass of champagne at a wedding.

Another myth worth busting is that of the teaspoon dangled in an open bottle to preserve the sparkle. Various tests, including one by the CIVC, have shown it has no effect whatsoever. Much better is to invest in a champagne stopper with hinged sides that clip on to the bottle. So long as you keep it in the fridge you can extend the life of an opened bottle over a long weekend and have a delicious apéritif every evening. And it goes without saying that every fridge should hold a bottle of champagne ready for a spontaneous celebration.

The rules on storage are the same with any wine – somewhere dark where the temperature is cool and constant. Champagne seems particularly sensitive to UV light, which explains the use of dark green glass or a cellophane wrapper in the case of Louis Roederer. When it comes to buying champagne, so long as the bottle hasn't sat too long under shop lights, you should be fine.

TOP LEFT Champagne bottles ranging from a tiddly quarter bottle for barely a sip to a party-sized Nebuchadnezzar with 15 litres of fizz.

LEFT Louis Roederer's *chef de cave* Jean-Baptiste Lécaillon inspecting one of his bottles by candle light in the cellars in Reims.

PART 2

THE HISTORY OF CHAMPAGNE

CHAMPAGNE HAS BEEN AT THE CROSSROADS OF WAR AND TRADE SINCE ATTILA THE HUN PAID AN UNWELCOME VISIT IN THE FIFTH CENTURY. THE REGION'S WINES ARE JUST AS OLD, BUT THE TRANSITION FROM STILL TO SPARKLING IS FAR MORE RECENT AND MIGHT NOT HAVE HAPPENED WITHOUT THE ENGLISH.

OPPOSITE The stained glass window in Reims Cathedral designed by Jacques Simon in 1954, showing the monks making champagne, and six of the champagne villages.

STARS IN THEIR EYES

THE WORLD'S MOST FAMOUS WINE WAS NOT INVENTED PER SE, IT WAS THE PRODUCT OF A GRADUAL EVOLUTION. YET THIS DID NOT STOP THE INDUSTRY FROM LATER CLAIMING THAT ONE MAN FROM THE MIDDLE YEARS OF THE LAST MILLENNIUM, WAS THE FOUNDING FATHER OF CHAMPAGNE.

"Come quickly. I'm drinking the stars!" cried the blind Benedictine monk, Dom Pérignon, having just created the most famous wine in the world. His moment of ecstasy was captured in stone in a life-size statue of him holding a foaming bottle of champagne. It stands on a plinth in the grounds of Moët & Chandon in Épernay in the heart of the Champagne region, and was used into the 1950s to advertise the Dom Pérignon brand. By 2007 that image had long gone, to be replaced by Claudia Schiffer, splayed across an unmade bed clutching a magnum-sized bottle, wearing fishnet tights, come-to-bed eyes and little else.

Quite what Dom Pérignon would have made of the German supermodel is anyone's guess, but one thing's for sure – the idea he invented sparkling champagne is pure fantasy. He wasn't even blind, and as for 'drinking the stars', the only reference to that came 200 years later in a print advert from the late nineteenth century. Yet he was certainly involved in the region's wines and did much to improve their quality as cellar master at the Abbaye

Saint-Pierre d'Hautvillers, just north of Épernay. It was one of his successors, Dom Grossard, who first propagated the myth about champagne in the 1820s.

Pérignon took up the post in 1668, aged 30, and remained there until his death in 1715. The crucial point to understand is that he and his fellow local winemakers produced champagne as a still wine. The presence of fizz in the finished product was proof that fermentation had not finished when it should have done. Bubbles were a fault to be stamped out, not least because they were dangerous. They were liable to shatter the relatively feeble bottles made of French glass, assuming any CO_2 hadn't already escaped through the *broquelet* – a primitive wooden stopper, dipped in oil and wrapped in hemp. Until the Champenois readopted that old Roman invention – the cork, sparkling wine was best avoided.

During his time at Hautvillers, Pérignon doubled the Abbey's vineyards to 20 hectares (50 acres) and focused on pinot noir

BELOW LEFT The star-struck monk Dom Pérignon having just invented sparkling champagne, or so the story goes. A life-size statue of him stands in the grounds of Moët & Chandon's headquarters in Épernay.

BELOW The famous Abbaye Saint-Pierre d'Hautvillers, just north of Épernay, where Dom Pérignon was cellar master until 1715. It was bought by Comte Pierre-Gabriel Chandon with its surrounding vineyards a century later.

among the various varieties grown in the region. He believed this noble grape, responsible for the great reds of Burgundy, was less volatile than white varieties and therefore less likely to re-ferment in the bottle or cask. He insisted the vines should be vigorously pruned to no more than a metre in height, and that the harvest be done with the utmost care so the grapes didn't split. Wine derives its colour from the skins of the grapes and he wanted to make a white pinot noir. Because horses were liable to become overexcited, he recommended using mules or donkeys to transport the grapes, which should be quickly pressed to minimise skin contact. Once the colour started to bleed through in the fourth or fifth pressing, the wine was to be rejected. As his successors at the Abbey noted, he was quite the perfectionist.

Champagne's name comes from *Campania*, which the Romans called this region east of Paris presumably because it reminded them of the open, rolling countryside of Campania, south of Rome. They planted the first vines here, though the earliest recorded vineyard was that of Saint Rémy in the fifth century. He was famous because his baptism of Clovis, the king of the Franks in AD 496, began the country's conversion to Christianity. It happened in Reims, the cathedral city and regional hub that became the spiritual capital of France like Canterbury in England. It was here that nearly all the French kings were crowned from Hugh Capet in 987 to Charles X in 1825, and this connection with royalty obviously boosted the reputation of the region and its wines. In the fifteenth century, not content with being just king of France, Francis I decreed that he was also *Roi d'Aÿ et de Gonesse* – Aÿ being a village east of Épernay whose vineyards were held in high regard and whose name was sometimes used to mean any wine from Champagne. The wines were otherwise referred to as *vins de Reims*, from the hillside of the so-called Montagne de Reims, or *vins de la rivière* from the Marne valley.

The River Marne flows west to join the Seine on the outskirts of Paris, which meant the wine could be shipped direct to the capital. In the other direction was the Rhineland, while to the north were the Low Countries and to the south, Switzerland. The Champagne region was thus strategically placed at a crossroads and there was a great deal of passing trade to be had. Unfortunately any merchant heading south would progress on to the warmer vineyards of Burgundy, where the red wines were undoubtedly better.

Winemakers in Champagne could manage only a pale imitation – deep pink at best and with a flavour that would have been quite acidic. As the climate cooled during the little ice age that began in the fifteenth century, the wines would have become even more tart. Some producers apparently added elderberries to boost the colour, though one wonders if many people were fooled. It seemed better to stick to making white wines, especially if you could vinify the clear juice of pinot noir without it being tinted by the skins, a trick supposedly pulled off by Dom Pérignon in Hautvillers.

Yet it was another Benedictine abbey in the village St Hilaire in the foothills of Limoux in southern France that lays claim to the first recorded trade in sparkling wines as early as 1531. They had access to corks to keep the bubbles in what became known as Blanquette de Limoux. Despite its 160-year head start, the wine has been somewhat eclipsed by champagne.

"Come quickly. I'm drinking the stars!"
DOM PÉRIGNON

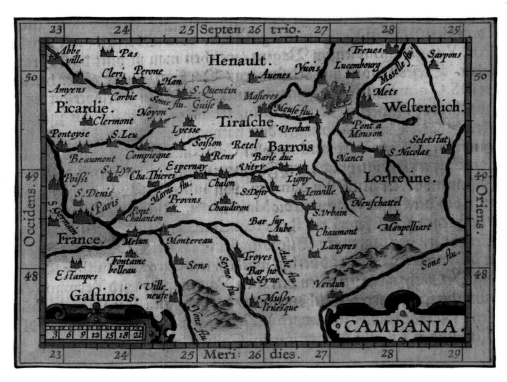

TOP Charles X was the last French monarch to be crowned in the Cathedral of Notre-Dame de Reims, (Our Lady of Reims) in 1825, bringing to an end a tradition that had lasted since the First Millennium.

ABOVE A sixteenth century map, drawn by the Flemish cartographer Abraham Ortelius, of 'Campania' as the Romans called the open, rolling countryside east of Paris.

AN ANGLO-FRENCH CREATION

SPARKLING CHAMPAGNE AS WE KNOW IT TODAY, OWES A DEBT TO A LONG-FORGOTTEN FIGURE ACROSS THE CHANNEL – A MAN WHO HAD NO LINKS TO THE WINE'S HOMELAND, BUT WHO UNDERSTOOD THE SCIENCE BEHIND THE BUBBLES.

So if it wasn't Dom Pérignon, who did put the fizz in champagne? Step forward Christopher Merret, an English physician and scientist born around 1615. He was a founding member of the Royal Society and had a particular interest in glass, which the English had been making in coal-fired furnaces since the early seventeenth century. They had been using wood as French glassmakers still did, but King James I had wanted to preserve the forests for shipbuilding. Using coal meant higher temperatures and therefore much stronger glass for making bottles. In those days wine was shipped in casks over to England, where it was bottled and stoppered with a cork. All things considered, sparkling wine was a much more viable proposition on the English side of the Channel.

In 1662 Merret delivered a paper to the Royal Society entitled 'Some Observations concerning the Ordering of Wines', which was unearthed by the wine writer Tom Stevenson fairly recently. It detailed the practice of adding sugar or molasses to a cask to make a wine taste 'brisk' and 'sparkling'. The yeast cells would emerge from their winter nap to feast on the sugar, burp CO_2 and die, though whether or not Merret understood this is unclear. But it was the first record of how to deliberately provoke a second fermentation and create a fizz, or *mousse,* in the wine. Indeed the first ever mention of sparkling champagne comes in a Restoration comedy, shortly afterwards, in 1676, *The Man of Mode* or *Sir Fopling Flutter,* by Sir George Etheredge.

> *To the mall and the park*
> *Where we love til 'tis dark,*
> *Then sparkling champaign*
> *Puts an end to their reign;*
> *It quickly recovers*
> *Poor languishing lovers,*
> *Make us frolick and gay, and*
> *drowns all our sorrows;*
> *But, alas! We relapse again on*
> *the morrow.*

So it seems the English were the first to enjoy the wine and its frolicsome effect, but to say they invented it is probably a stretch. It was, after all, the Champenois who made the wine with its occasionally unfermented yeast, and to be honest it wasn't really an invention at all, more a very slow evolution that took a century and a half. Let us just say, in the spirit of the Entente Cordiale, that champagne was an Anglo-French creation, and that the world is all the better for it. But whatever the truth, back in the vineyards of Champagne it was certainly no

overnight conversion from still wine to full-on fizz.

It was only in the third edition of the posthumous memoir about Dom Pérignon that a note was added claiming 'a credible witness' had seen him lace his wines with a mixture of peaches, nuts and sugar candy to encourage the *mousse.* The poor monk would have been turning in his grave. As the French writer Raymond Dumay put it: "He knew of no enemy more dangerous than a wine which 'worked', that is to say a wine which, despite everything, was determined to bubble for the whole of its life." Sparkling champagne was considered the devil's wine for the way it could blow up in your face, or set off a chain reaction in the cellar and destroy hundreds of bottles. Nor was it considered a serious wine. "A wine will turn frothy particularly if it is strong and green … froth is suitable only for chocolate, beer or whipped cream," wrote the wine merchant Bertin de Rocheret in 1726. Among connoisseurs, and most winemakers in Champagne, that view endured throughout the eighteenth century.

Yet among London's café society and the court of Versailles in France, the capricious nature of those bubbles must have enhanced the wine's appeal. There was something so haphazard

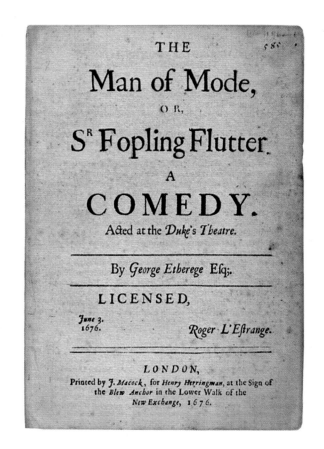

THE
Man of Mode,
OR,
Sᴿ Fopling Flutter.
A
COMEDY.
Acted at the *Duke's* Theatre.

By *George Etherege* Esq;.

LICENSED,
June 3.
1676.
Roger L'Eſtrange.

LONDON,
Printed by *J. Macock,* for *Henry Herringman,* at the Sign of the *Blew Anchor* in the Lower Walk of the *New Exchange,* 1676.

ABOVE Christopher Merret, the English physician and scientist who wrote the first ever paper on how to deliberately cause wines to sparkle with the addition of sugar. It was presented to the Royal Society in 1662.

LEFT The first ever mention of sparkling champagne on either side of the Channel appeared in this Restoration comedy by George Etheridge, first performed in London in 1676.

and magical about the sparkle and whether it would happen at all. As the cork was eased from the bottle – would there be a deathly sigh or an exhilarating pop and rush of foam? Perhaps for some the risk of the bottle exploding like a grenade added an extra frisson of excitement.

In England, champagne had its very own ambassador in the Marquis de St Evremond, who had been exiled to London in 1662. He was an aesthete and friend of Charles II, who as a joke made him warden of Duck Island in the pond in St James' Park and paid him an annual stipend of £300 – a fortune in those days. But Evremond was not a proponent of sparkling champagne. For him it was invariably a still wine, be it red from pinot noir grown on the slopes of the Montagne de Reims, or white from top villages like Hautvillers and Sillery.

The Marquis de Sillery and his descendants owned a 50-hectare estate which they supplemented with other vineyards to create a blend and arguably the first real brand of champagne, though never a sparkling one. It was particularly prized in Britain, but to secure an allocation you needed contacts, which is where Evremond came in. Meanwhile, back in France, the still red wines of champagne had suffered a blow when King Louis XIV's doctor persuaded him in 1695 to switch to Burgundy for the sake of his health. For the next 50 years the Champenois fought a losing battle with the Burgundians over who could produce the best red wine from pinot noir.

Others saw it more as a rosé, or 'clairet', whose colour was often referred to as partridge eye or onion skin, while some winemakers favoured Dom Pérignon's approach of minimal skin contact for the clearest, palest wines. As for those occasional rogue bottles that sparkled, the first mention in France referred to a *mousse argentine*, or silvery fizz, in 1712. At the time it seemed most unlikely it would ever catch on.

RIGHT Jean-François de Troy's *Le Déjeuner d'huîtres* (The Oyster Lunch, 1735) is believed to be the first time champagne bottles appeared in a painting. It could not have been a more glamorous debut.

ABOVE A noted bon viveur and wit, the Marquis de St Evremond was champagne's first unofficial ambassador in England, where he was exiled in 1662. For Evremond, however, champagne was invariably a still wine.

RIGHT The court of Charles II was the most hedonistic in English history – at least, as depicted in this satirical print by John Leech from *The Comic History of England* (1850).

Evening Party-Time of Charles II

FRIVOLOUS FIZZ

SPARKLING CHAMPAGNE RECEIVED A BOOST IN FRANCE UNDER THE PLAYFUL PHILIPPE, DUKE OF ORLÉANS, WHO SUCCEEDED THE SOMEWHAT AUSTERE LOUIS XIV AS REGENT IN 1715. THE FRENCH NOBILITY TOOK TO THIS NEW VICE DURING THE REGENCY, FOLLOWING IN THE FOOTSTEPS OF THEIR KINDRED SPIRITS IN ENGLAND.

On which note, it's impossible to know how many casks were being shipped to the *bon viveurs* Sir Fopling Flutter, and his ilk in London, and sweetened up to provoke a secondary fermentation, but there was certainly a tradition of doctoring wines. Port and sherry were invariably fortified to survive the rough crossing across the Bay of Biscay, by Britain's ex-pat wine trade in Porto and Jerez. According to Nicholas Faith in *The Story of Champagne*, only the wines of Burgundy and Champagne arrived here in their natural state. They didn't need fortifying for the 20-mile crossing over the Channel, though in the case of champagne it was best to bottle the wines quickly.

Winemakers in Champagne were soon in a better position to attempt to make sparkling wines if they wished to do so. A new glassworks was established in the nearby forest of Argonne to produce stronger bottles, and the use of cork stoppers, first introduced by the Romans, became widespread again. The law that theoretically banned the transport of bottled wine outside Champagne, except for the privileged few, was repealed in 1728. And seven years later, the quality and weight of the bottles was fixed by a royal decree which also stipulated that the cork should be tied on with a piece of string. In the meantime Nicolas Ruinart, a local wool merchant, established the first Champagne House in Épernay in 1729.

The balance of power in the region's wine trade was shifting. Reims, whose agents, or *courtiers*, had once enjoyed a monopoly, was losing out to Épernay, whose merchants began supplying European markets direct. In the mid-eighteenth century the strongest demand came from the Low Countries and the many German courts that slavishly followed the fashions of Versailles. After Ruinart, others began setting up shop. There was Claude Moët, a local vineyard owner who established his family firm in Épernay in 1743, and Florens-Louis Heidsieck, the first of the German merchants to arrive. His compatriots were to play a major role in the history of champagne in the nineteenth century.

Yet most producers remained sceptical of this frivolous new fad

BELOW LEFT The French Regent, Philip Duke of Orleans, is depicted here by Nicolas de Largillie as Bacchus, the Roman god of wine – a clear sign that the good times were back after his succession from Louis XIV in 1715.

BELOW The amount of wine that was being shipped into England from France is clear in this satirical print from 1757, "Humbly address'd to the laudable association of anti-gallicans".

for fizz. Nicolas Bidet, born in 1709, a local author of various wine books, was convinced it was ruining the region's reputation as a source of good-quality still wines. You can almost hear the sneer in the following passage: "The vivacity, the exuberance of Champagne's wines, known in Paris only under the name of sparkling wine, this froth, this creamy mousse so dear to the heart of the ladies … is responsible." There were various degrees of frothiness starting with the *tisane de champagne*, which barely bubbled at all, through *pétillant* to *demi-mousseux* that was similar to a *crémant* or *frizzante* style of Prosecco. While sparkliest of all was the *saute-bouchon*, or 'cork jumper', though even this would have contained about half the pressure of today's bottles.

Whether or not it was worth ignoring Bidet's distain, there was no consensus among producers where the bubbles came from. The white grapes grown on the chalky soils of the Côtes des Blancs, south of Épernay, now almost exclusively planted with chardonnay, seemed especially prone to it. So too were wines that were particularly green and acidic. Some thought it was down to the temperature of the cellars where the bottles were kept, others blamed the cycles of the moon. But whatever the cause, there were sound, practical reasons for producers not to indulge the market for them. "At the beginning of the eighteenth century they were already aware of the more frequent accidents and the principal technical troubles found with sparkling wine," wrote Armand de Maizière in his book on the origins of the champagne trade, published in 1848. "… invariably some recalcitrant bottles did not sparkle at all

… [while others] exploded with a high-pitched crack enough to break their neighbours: explosive breakages in otherwise recalcitrant bottles; corks which proved defective either because of the cork itself, or because they were simply too small: wines which were sick because of thickness, grease, bitterness, acidity" … and so on. It was clearly far safer to stick to the tranquillity of still wines, and hope the fashion for bubbles would soon pop.

Winemakers could expect to lose one-third to one-half of their bottles every year, according to one eighteenth-century figure in the trade. He believed such wastage bumped up the price of sparkling champagne to eight times its true value. Of course the high price only fuelled the desire among its well-heeled clientele, and this became a recurrent theme in the history of champagne and the creation of luxury brands. Being expensive and therefore exclusive was the perfect start for what became a liquid status symbol as the reason for the high price slowly shifted from the cost of production to the cost of marketing.

Deluxe brands were way in the distance, however, as the Ancien Régime began to crumble in the late eighteenth century. While the working-class *sans-culottes* in Paris were storming the Bastille in 1789, the peasant farmers of Champagne were complaining they lived on nothing but bread soaked in salt water. However much their fate improved after the French Revolution, the immediate beneficiaries were the merchants. As the old estates belonging to the monasteries or local families like the Marquis de Sillery were broken up into small parcels, the merchants' names evolved into brands.

ABOVE LEFT The storming of the Bastille, on 14 July 1789. Louis XVI, on hearing of the news, asked the Duc de Liancourt: "Is this a revolt?" "No, Sir," came the famous reply. "This is a revolution."

TOP Nicolas Ruinart, founder of the oldest established Champagne House in 1729. He was apparently inspired by his uncle Dom Thierry Ruinart to believe there was a future for 'wine with bubbles'.

ABOVE Claude Moët was a grower and winemaker who was supplying the court at Versailles before setting up his own Champagne House in 1743.

CHAMPAGNE COMES OF AGE

FRANCE CHANGED IRREVOCABLY ON 14 JULY 1789, THE DAY OF THE REVOLUTION. YET IT WAS A CASE OF *PLUS ÇA CHANGE, PLUS C'EST LA MÊME CHOSE*, OR BUSINESS AS USUAL, FOR THE NASCENT CHAMPAGNE INDUSTRY AS IT ADAPTED TO LIFE UNDER THE NEW REGIME.

Sales of champagne doubled in the latter part of the eighteenth century, and stood at 288,000 bottles in the year before the Revolution in 1789. How much was sparkling is hard to say, but probably no more than one-tenth. It is also unclear how much was still being shipped in cask, whether to be drunk as a still wine or deliberately re-fermented into fizz with a few spoonfuls of sugar. Either way, by 1794, the Napoleonic Wars had pushed up the price of champagne to 90 shillings a case, double that of any other wine.

The Moët family certainly got off to a good start under the new regime when Jean-Rémy Moët was appointed mayor of Épernay in 1792. Seven years later a certain François-Marie Clicquot married Barbe-Nicole Ponsardin secretly in a cellar. According to legend, the priest gave the happy couple a book about Dom Pérignon.

Clicquot's father was a local banker and tradesman who owned a vineyard near the delightfully named village of Bouzy, east of Épernay, and had a small winery there. Ponsardin was even better connected. Her father was a successful textile merchant turned Jacobin whom Napoleon made mayor of Reims.

In 1805 M. Clicquot died, leaving a three-year-old daughter, a business that involved banking, wool and champagne, and a 27-year-old widow. As Veuve Clicquot, Barbe-Nicole was to have a huge impact on champagne, and her own brand in particular. Given the contemporary mores about women staying at home, something the Napoleonic Code upheld, being a widow may have been her salvation. She realised they were the "only women granted the social freedom to run their own affairs". The

BELOW The Emperor Napoleon striking a classic pose in the cellars of his close friend Jean-Rémy Moët in July 1807. As well as running his champagne business, Moët was mayor of Épernay.

champagne side of the business had been flourishing under her late husband, with sales up from 8,000 bottles in 1796 to 60,000 in 1804. But with the Royal Navy tightening its blockade as the war in Europe continued, the prospects looked grim.

Sales of Veuve Clicquot dropped to 10,000 bottles a year, and her erstwhile business partner, Alexandre Fourneaux, gave up. "Business terribly stagnant," wrote her head salesman, Louis Bohne, in 1810. "No sea traffic due to the English fleet. In Vienna the nobility has no money to pay tradesmen not having sold any wheat for three years. Prices are plummeting." One assumes he was referring to sparkling champagne, which was still a very different drink to what we enjoy today. It tended to be cloudy and, although you could decant it into a new bottle you risked losing much of the sparkle. It was at least 10 times sweeter than a modern-style Brut champagne, and had none of those elegant little bubbles to tickle your nose. The bubbles were fat and gassy like those on a pint of beer, and Madame Clicquot called them 'toad's eyes'.

She set about perfecting the art of *remuage*, with her cellar master, Antoine-Aloys de Muller. He cut slanting holes in an old desk, or *pupitre*, into which the bottles were placed neck first for four months of riddling. With a daily quarter-turn and a quick jiggle, the lees eventually collected behind the cork. Keeping the bottle at an angle, the cork and sediment were fired into a bucket, the bottle flipped round, topped up with the sugary *liqueur de tirage*, and quickly recorked. Corks were originally inserted by the workers using their teeth, apparently, which must have kept the local dentists busy. In time producers progressed to using a hammer and then a corking machine in 1827.

"Spring water is not as clear," boasted Louis Bohne about the improved champagne, though Madame Clicquot failed to keep the method secret from her rivals. In 1811 a bright comet streaked across the skies above Champagne, heralding the best vintage anyone could recall. The Russians were developing a taste for fizz, only for the Czar to ban French wine imports in 1812. Scenting an opportunity, Bohne sailed for Königsberg on the Prussian coast and managed to pre-sell his consignment before reaching St Petersburg. "All their tongues are hanging out to taste it," he wrote of the famed 'Vin de la Comète', "and if it's as good as it is beautiful, they will all end up loving me."

Other merchants were eyeing up the Russian market. In 1812 Charles-Henri Heidsieck rode into Moscow on a white stallion ahead of Napoleon's advancing army with champagne to sell to the victor, whoever that might be. Two years later Russian and Prussian troops had swept into France and captured Reims. With Cossacks laying waste to the vineyards and plundering bottles of champagne, Madame Clicquot and others were frantically bricking up their cellars. It was around this time that the first cavalry officer sliced open a bottle with his sabre, in what became known as *sabrage*. Whether he was a Cossack or a dashing French hussar is unclear, but it certainly added to the glamour of champagne. During the protracted negotiations of the Congress of Vienna, which lasted from September 1814 through to the following June and the Battle of Waterloo, the wine was served at countless receptions and parties. Its bond with celebration and good times was being cemented.

While Veuve Clicquot and later Roederer secured their grip on Russia, which was soon the second biggest export market after Britain, new Champagne Houses were popping up in Épernay and Reims. Henriot opened in 1808, followed by Perrier-Jouët and Laurent-Perrier a few years later, then Mumm and Bollinger in

the 1820s, and Pommery and others a decade later. The old Rue de Châlons in Épernay was fast becoming the grand Avenue de Champagne. By 1848, a book on the origins of champagne was claiming that: "Sparkling wines have made fortunes for twenty merchants [and] ensure an honest living for a hundred more." Champagne was coming of age.

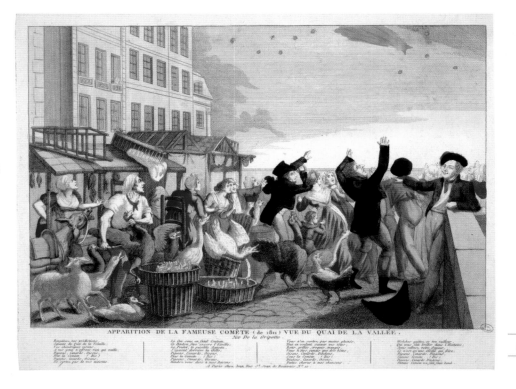

APPARITION DE LA FAMEUSE COMÈTE (de 1811) VUE DU QUAI DE LA VALLÉE.
Air De la Gripotte

TOP Stallholders on the Quai de la Vallée, on the banks of the Seine in Paris, gaze at the Great Comet of 1811. In Champagne, it heralded one of the best vintages for years.

ABOVE The protracted negotiations of the Congress of Vienna (1814–15) were an attempt to redraw Europe's boundaries and achieve a lasting peace after the Napoleonic wars.

IN THE EARLY 1800s JEAN-ANTOINE CHAPTAL, A PHYSICIAN AND NAPOLEON BONAPARTE'S INTERIOR MINISTER, ADVOCATED SUGAR AS A CURE FOR GREEN, UNRIPE WINES IN FRANCE'S COOLER VINEYARD REGIONS LIKE CHAMPAGNE.

Adding sugar boosts the alcoholic strength and amount of fizz in the case of sparkling wine, but the question was how much to add before the bottles exploded. This was resolved to a large extent by André François, a local chemist who devised a scientific formula in 1836.

Breakages were reduced to around 5%, and it allowed producers to safely increase the pressure in the bottle halfway towards the full-on fizz of today. Much more important, it made sparkling champagne a truly viable business for the first time. It attracted a growing crowd of commercially savvy producers. There were the Germans like Krug, Deutz, Mumm and Bollinger, and a number of entrepreneurial French Houses including Mercier and Pommery, both founded in 1858. This new generation of merchants wasted no time in carving out global markets and building their brands. Some of the original Champenois like the Comte de Villermot thought it vulgar to put one's name on a label, but that wasn't an issue for his son-in-law Jacques Bollinger.

By 1870 production had reached 20 million bottles from barely a million at the start of the century. Almost every inch of the Marne's traditional slopes was now carpeted with vines. Tastes varied within different markets, with the prize for the sweetest tooth going to Russia. According to the drinks journalist Patrick Schmitt: "There are stories of Russian Czars drinking it with 200 grams per litre of sugar which is more than a can of Coke." Roederer became the 'Official Supplier to the Imperial Court of Russia', for which it created the famous sweet *cuvée* Cristal in 1876.

Mainland Europe, including France, preferred their champagne considerably sweeter than today because it was served with the pudding or afterwards as a toast. In Britain it was drunk as an apéritif, since after-dinner drinking favoured sweet, fortified wines like Port and Madeira. Portuguese wines had enjoyed a tax advantage over French wines ever since the Methuen Treaty of 1703, which the British Chancellor, William Gladstone, corrected only in 1860. Champagne remained a drink to aspire to with prices to match, but it was increasingly within reach of the middle classes, and UK sales trebled over the next 30 years. By 1900 40% of the

BELOW LEFT Veuve Madame Pommery's imposing marble-clad champagne factory in Reims designed by the architect Alphonse Gosset in 1882.

BELOW Czar Nicholas II, the last Emperor of Russia, with his wife Alexandra, at a New Year's Day reception in 1897. The Russian court was awash with champagne, particularly the syrupy-sweet cuvées of Roederer and Veuve Clicquot.

RIGHT Ever the showman, Eugène Mercier, spent 15 years building his 'Cathedral of Champagne' – the world's largest barrel. In 1889 it was towed by 24 oxen and 18 horses from Épernay to Paris for the Second World Fair.

BELOW A trio of highly ornate champagne flutes from the 1830s.

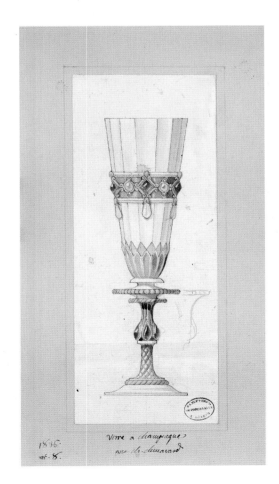

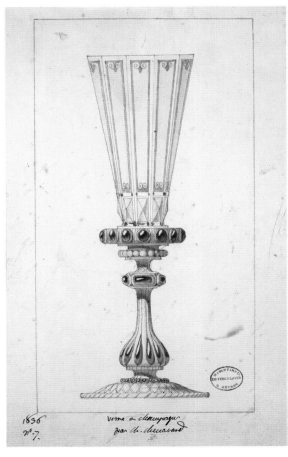

Souvenir de l'Exposition Universelle
PALAIS DE L'ALIMENTATION

GROS TONNEAU CONTENANT 200,000 BOU...

Envoyé tout monté à Paris sur un char traîné par **24 Bœufs**

Exposé par **MM. MERCIER & CIE**, Négociants en Vins de Champagne à

Hors Concours — Membre du Jury

1889

ILLES

rnay (Marne)

wine's entire production, or 10.75 million bottles, were consumed by the Brits, an amount not exceeded until the 1970s.

Clicquot and Heidsieck were shipping wines to England labelled 'Dry' as early as 1857, followed by 'Very Dry' from Bollinger in 1868. Other terms like 'Extra Sec' or 'Extra Dry' were used as tastes for richer styles of champagne began to fade. Madame Pommery, an astute businesswoman and widow very much in the mould of Veuve Clicquot, launched the first Brut champagne in 1874, having opened a London office 13 years earlier. For decades Pommery was the UK's most popular champagne, though 'Brut' remained a minority interest for some time.

The devastating Franco-Prussian War of 1870 saw the vineyards overrun, Paris under siege and the end of Napoleon III's rule. When the Prussians withrew, Champagne entered a golden age that was to last until 1914. After the horrors of the First World War, the era was given the rose-tinted title of the Belle Époque – a halcyon period of peace and prosperity when the arts and science flourished. This was the time of Toulouse-Lautrec, Maxim's and the Folies Bergère when the bourgeoisie embraced the fashions of Parisian high society, or 'Le Tout-Paris', and dined out on a rising tide of champagne. The drink's image was everywhere from posters in the Metro to adverts in magazines, all seeking to capture the essential joie de vivre in those bubbles. Sex was a recurrent theme. One brand featured a crusty old gent on all fours fumbling to attach a garter to the leg of a young woman, presumably his mistress. A free pair of garters was offered with every bottle.

As Paris prepared for the Universal Exhibition in 1889, with its 'temporary' metal entrance – the Eiffel Tower, Eugène Mercier had the world's biggest barrel filled with champagne and towed to the city by 24 white oxen. News of the stunt was reported as far afield as San Francisco. Paris, with its *fin de siècle* decadence and glamour, was more about image than sales for the big Champagne Houses whose sights were on burgeoning export markets like America. Charles Heidsieck, the original 'Champagne Charlie', first crossed the Atlantic back in 1852 and ended up being captured by Union troops in the American Civil War. Within a decade of the war's ending in 1865, US exports were approaching 400,000 bottles, led by Piper-Heidsieck. In 1876, Mumm released Cordon Rouge, which was an instant hit in France and easy to remember for visiting tourists due to its striking red sash across the label. Five years later it was launched in the States and spread fast through nightclubs, restaurants and brothels. It flowed through New Orleans jazz clubs and inspired the 'Cordon Rouge Gallop' – a prelude to rap music's embrace of Cognac a century later and the Busta Rhymes hit 'Pass the Courvoisier'. By 1903 the biggest brand in the States was Moët & Chandon's White Seal with sales of over 1.2 million bottles, a quarter of Moët's entire production.

LEFT Mercier's giant barrel held the equivalent of 200,000 bottles of wine and weighed so much that two bridges collapsed on its journey to Paris in 1889.

OPPOSITE Pierre Bonnard's famous poster with its frothing tide of fizz appeared all over Paris in the spring of 1891.

LEFT "Gentlemen!! Do you wish to conquer hearts!" declares this saucy poster for a long forgotten brand. Somehow, it's clear the coquettish lady with the black tights and splayed legs is not his wife.

REVOLUTION AND STRIFE

CHAMPAGNE ENTERED THE TWENTIETH CENTURY WITH GLOBAL SALES APPROACHING 35 MILLION BOTTLES, AND DEMAND RISING AT HOME AND ABROAD. IT SEEMED THE BEST OF ALL POSSIBLE WORLDS – YET ALL WAS NOT WELL BEHIND THE SCENES.

The name of 'champagne' was being traduced on a global scale, and within Champagne unscrupulous producers were undercutting the growers, or *vignerons*, by buying cheap base wine from the South. Meanwhile a tiny, sap-sucking aphid called phylloxera was slowly munching its way northwards through the vineyards of France.

In 1842, Charles Dickens encountered American 'champagne' made from sweetened turnips. Closer to home, there were 'champagnes' from the Loire, Burgundy, Italy and Spain. The campaign to stamp out these imposters led to the Union des Maisons de Champagne (UMC), founded in 1882. Among its aims were to: 'prevent the "Champagne" name from being misused across the world'. The issue was whether it was really a process or a region. When Josep Raventós, the pioneer of Spanish cava, promoted his wine as Cordoníu Champagne, was he ripping off the French or using a commonly understood term? The longer Cordoníu and others did so, the greater the risk that champagne would become as generic as London Dry gin or Cheddar cheese.

Less contentious was the obvious opportunism of those producers who hired anyone with the right surname, from former cavalry officer Paul Ruinart to Strasbourg waiter Théophile Roederer. There was also Clicquot 'champagne' from Hungary, and a town in America that was rechristened Reims by a local producer. In Europe, the first framework for protecting a wine's geographic origin was established in 1890, though it took until 1905 to become law in France, paving the way for the *appellation contrôlée*

system. When the issue came to the US courts, the UMC refused to pay for an American lawyer demanding US$15,000 if he lost and US$50,000 if he won. It's a decision that has haunted them ever since, given American stores still stock Californian champagne despite howls of protest from the French.

In 1890, phylloxera finally reached Champagne nearly 30 years after it was first spotted in southern France. It had devastated Bordeaux and other regions, yet the Champenois were ill prepared and complacent. At first the chalky soils seemed to offer protection and by 1898 only 50 hectares were affected. Within a decade, however, more than 30% of the Marne's vineyards had been wiped out. The solution – that of grafting the vines on to American rootstock – was already known, but it involved huge effort and expense. With global demand for champagne rising, merchants were forced further afield to source their base wine. Much was coming from the nearby Aube region halfway to Burgundy, while some was simply the cheapest plonk from the Midi.

Every autumn barrels of 'foreign' wine piled up at Épernay station while grape prices fell and the champagne chatelaines grew ever richer. In 1890 René Lamarre, the original champagne socialist, urged his 18,000 fellow *vignerons* to form a giant co-operative and share the riches, leaving the merchants with nothing. "Phylloxera isn't the only parasite in our vineyards," declared his pamphlet *La Révolution Champenoise*. He accused the merchants of being interested only in their brands, and predicted: "Within ten years we will no longer recognise the name of champagne."

BELOW LEFT *Phylloxera*, the microscopic aphid that blighted Europe's vineyards in the nineteenth century reached Champagne in 1890. It has never been eradicated, but merely held in check by grafting the vines onto American rootstock.

BELOW If imitation be the sincerest form of flattery, the Champenois refused to be flattered as they embarked on decades of litigation to stamp out imposters including this Spanish lookalike.

Producers in the Aube were desperate to join Champagne, since Burgundy didn't want them and their trade with Paris had been lost to cheaper wines from the Midi. In 1908 official sales of champagne were almost 33 million bottles, while the Marne produced enough for just 16 million. That year the government set the boundaries of Champagne for the first time, excluding the Aube. "They've slit our throats," cried one local in despair. "If we're not part of Champagne, what are we? Part of the moon?"

Unfortunately most of the Aube was planted with local grapes of the Beaujolais variety, Gamay, which doesn't make good sparkling wine. A second government edict in February 1911 kept them out of Champagne, provoking mass demonstrations in the region. Local *vignerons* marched through the streets, armed with the hoes, or *fousseux*, they used to weed their vineyards. "Be strong and united," urged their leader Gaston Cheq, "there will be a gold mine ahead for you."

Two months later the government panicked and annulled the

1908 law, allowing the Aube to join Champagne and provoking an immediate, violent backlash in the Marne. It was the final straw after the worst harvest on record with truly pitiful yields. "One *vigneron* managed to make only a single bottle of wine, and that to keep as a souvenir," wrote Don and Petie Kladstrup in *Champagne – How the World's Most Glamorous Wine Triumphed Over War and Hard Times*. "Another picked so few grapes that all she could do was make a tart."

On the night of 11 April 1911, within hours of the government's decision, the Marne vineyards echoed to the sound of drums and bugles. The mob wreaked terror from one village to the next, burning cars, overturning trucks, breaking into cellars and smashing casks. Some 35,000 troops were drafted in overnight to quell the riot, but when the growers were blocked from entering Épernay, they attacked the nearby village of Aÿ. Buildings and vineyards were set on fire, while the streets flowed with wine. By 13 April it was all over, and amazingly no one had been killed.

BELOW A government edict excluding the Aube from the magic appellation of champagne, sparked protests across the region in the spring of 1911. "If we're not part of Champagne," cried one furious *vigneron*, "What are we? Part of the moon?"

WORLD WAR BLUES

THE CONFLICT THAT LED TO THE CHAMPAGNE RIOTS SOON BECAME NOTHING MORE THAN 'A LITTLE LOCAL DIFFICULTY' WHEN COMPARED TO WHAT DEVELOPED DURING THE SUMMER OF 1914. WITHIN MONTHS THE REGION FOUND ITSELF CAUGHT IN THECROSSFIRE OF THE WAR TO END ALL WARS.

To maintain the peace after the Champagne riots, tens of thousands of troops were drafted into the region, and remained there until the harvest. After a spate of dismal vintages, 1911 saw a bumper harvest, and the authorities took advantage of the optimistic mood to declare the Aube could also produce champagne. It was to be called *Champagne deuxième zone*, or second division. Everyone knew it was a temporary fix, and the government was debating the issue yet again, when the assassination of Archduke Franz Ferdinand in Sarajevo in June 1914 changed everything.

Germany declared war on 3 August, and swept through the Low Countries into France in accordance with the Schlieffen Plan for a quick, decisive victory. Within weeks the people of Reims could hear the enemy's big guns approaching, and on 4 September the city was captured, followed by Épernay a day later. Part of the German army had crossed the River Marne and was within striking distance of Paris. The French government had fled to Bordeaux, leaving General Joseph Gallieni to defend the capital. Around midnight on 6 September he ordered Parisian taxi drivers to assemble in front of

Les Invalides and ferry some 6,000 French troops to the front.

The convoy made its way east with headlights blacked out and meters running in time-honoured taxi tradition. The Battle of the Marne lasted a week and left an estimated half a million soldiers dead or wounded. The Germans retreated after their week-long occupation of Reims, to face the Allied forces across no man's land. The war that was supposed to be over by Christmas was now bogged down in the trenches that ran from the North Sea to Switzerland. The frontline cut through Champagne, and German guns in the hills beyond Reims continued to pound the city for the rest of the war.

The famous Reims Cathedral where so many French kings had been crowned was spared at first, but soon shells rained down reducing it to a burnt-out shell. This image became an important piece of anti-German propaganda, symbolising the barbarity of the Bosch. Many fled the city, while those who stayed disappeared into the *crayères*, the labyrinthine network of champagne tunnels. They were far more than just a refuge from German bombs like

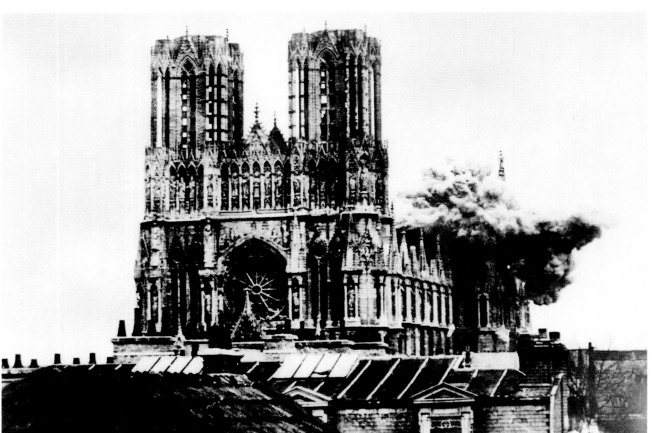

ABOVE A World War One cartoon by Bernard Partridge, "A champagne counter-offensive", showing the region's fightback against the German invading army.

LEFT Notre-Dames de Reims was an early casualty of World War One, with the first shells landing on 20 September 1914. The north tower caught fire and molten lead from the roof poured through the stone gargoyles.

the London Underground would be during the Blitz of the 1940s, and became a surreal subterranean universe that reflected life above ground before the war. There were shops, hospitals, church services, school lessons and even a few cows to provide milk. The tunnels "were bomb-proof and, when warmed with electricity or fuel stoves, proved by no means uncomfortable to live in," wrote Patrick Forbes in *Champagne: The Wine, the Land and the People*. "In fact many people," he concluded, "were so content underground that they did not come up for months at a time, and in certain cases for as long as two years." Reims was eventually evacuated, but when people returned there were just 40 houses still standing.

Despite the shelling and lack of manpower, grapes were picked every harvest throughout the war to produce a small, heroic vintage. Champagne Houses were badly shelled, including Ruinart, Lanson and Pommery. Meanwhile Mumm was seized by the French state because its owner, Hermann von Mumm, was interned in Brittany, having failed to take out French citizenship in time. As for the vineyards, 40% had been put out of action by shelling, gas and that seemingly indestructible aphid, phylloxera.

In 1919 a new French law reaffirmed the boundary of Champagne and decreed that only grapes grown in the region could be used. Reims was quickly rebuilt and the domestic trade picked up, at least in Paris with the Jazz Age in full swing. Legitimate trade with the States was snuffed out by Prohibition in 1920, though the 13 'dry' years saw at least 71 million bottles of champagne consumed according to a 'best guess estimate' by Don and Petie Kladstrup. Their book gives a vivid account of Jean-Charles Heidsieck's adventures supplying the underworld with fizz. The

biggest risks were for the middlemen or rum-runners, while a bonus for suppliers like Heidsieck was the fact you didn't pay a cent of sales tax.

A year after Prohibition ended in 1933, Champagne enjoyed one of its best vintages for decades. Unfortunately the West was in the grip of the Great Depression and trade, both domestic and export, had collapsed. Grape prices fell from over 10 francs per kilo in 1926 to just 50 centimes and were barely worth picking. Producers decided to invoke the spirit of Dom Pérignon, by then a somewhat forgotten figure, and announced the 250th anniversary of the monk's 'invention' of champagne. Of more lasting impact was Dom Pérignon the brand, the first out and out luxury vintage champagne, released by Moët & Chandon in 1935.

Four years later the world was back at war, only this time the Champenois had eight months to hide thousands of bottles before the German invasion began in May 1940. The Nazis appointed Otto Klaebisch as *weinführer*, to extract as much champagne and profit as possible, while representing the industry was Count Robert-Jean de Vogüé, head of Moët & Chandon. He was also chief of the political wing of the French Resistance in eastern France and narrowly escaped the death penalty in 1943. There were countless tales of heroism, and the tunnels of many Champagne Houses were used to hide Resistance fighters and stash arms dropped by the Allies. But as a region, the damage was nothing compared to the previous conflict. According to Nicholas Faith in *The Story of Champagne*, there were just a couple of air raids and a few bombs accidentally dropped on Aÿ by an American airman, during the entire war.

FAR LEFT Comte Robert-Jean de Vogüé, Moët & Chandon's inspirational boss and industry leader during the German occupation in World War II. He escaped the death sentence and survived years in the notorious Ziegenhain labour camp.

LEFT "I confirm I have arrived safely" ran the caption on this cartoon postcard of two GIs soaking up the nightlife in Paris after the city's liberation in August 1944.

THE ASCENDANCE OF CHAMPAGNE

THE FIRST HALF OF THE TWENTIETH CENTURY WAS DIFFICULT NOT ONLY FOR CHAMPAGNE BUT THE WORLD IN GENERAL. SUCH WAS THE IMPACT OF TWO WORLD WARS, THE GREAT DEPRESSION AND US PROHIBITION THAT CHAMPAGNE SALES RECOVERED TO THEIR 1913 LEVEL OF 35 MILLION BOTTLES ONLY IN THE MID-1950S.

During this period the industry consolidated and some once famous names disappeared, while many of the growers had joined co-operatives owned by their members. At first the co-ops produced only base wine, or *vin clair*, but under pressure to do more, they merged into larger unions of co-operatives where they had the scale to invest in cellars and bottling lines. In time they began supplying the supermarkets with own-brand champagne, or selling it on the open market in a practice known as *sur latte*.

The *latte* are the thin wooden strips between the rows of bottles ageing in the cellar, and wines sold *sur latte* are in unlabelled bottles yet to be disgorged. They are bought by merchants who will slap on a label as though they were the producer, having done nothing more than disgorge the wines and decide on the level of *dosage*. Like those tartan rugs from Pakistan labelled 'hand-finished in Scotland', there's a distinct whiff of deception about *sur latte* with the consumer left blissfully unaware. It is the real commodity end of the champagne trade, and despite repeated calls for a ban, it continues to this day.

Out of the war came the Comité Interprofessionel du vin de Champagne, or CIVC, founded in 1941. Before each harvest it would set grape prices according to the strength of the market and whether or not the vineyards were rated grands crus, premier crus or deuxième crus. Since 1990 this rigid system was replaced with a free-trade negotiation between the Champagne Houses and the growers. The CIVC is also charged with providing technical support, enforcing the rules, promoting the wines and the region, and protecting the champagne 'brand'. The first big victory in the courts was over Spanish 'champagne' in the 1950s. Since then, with the exception of a few 'champagne' brands in the US, the CIVC's lawyers have gradually squeezed out other imposters while clamping down on 'parasite products' from 'champagne' soaps to Babycham. Perhaps their greatest coup was having the expression *méthode champenoise* banned in the EU in 1992. At a stroke there was clear blue water between champagne and that woefully generic term – sparkling wine.

The first big post-war market to emerge took everyone by surprise. Domestic consumption had grown five-fold by the late 1970s and accounted for two-thirds of all champagne, in complete contrast to the start of the century. Almost half the wine was coming from the grower producers, or *récoltant manipulant*s,

BELOW LEFT In the smaller Champagne Houses automation was slow to arrive and staff at Pommery's cellars, near Reims were still wrapping the bottles of champagne by hand in 1956.

BELOW Bottles lying *sur latte* (on slats) in the Taittinger cellars. The corks apart, there are no labels attached to the bottles so the seller will, after the disgorgement, put it on the market as if they were the makers.

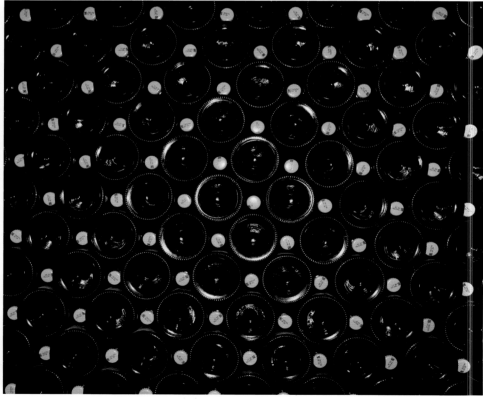

whom the French, and especially the Parisians, loved to buy from. For these small producers it meant cash in hand and no need to go through a costly distribution chain, while for the consumer it was a chance to deal direct with the family who made the champagne, or so it seemed. In reality the wine was often the non-vintage Brut from the local co-op to which the grower belonged. He had simply labelled some stock that he had bought, that possibly contained one or two of his grapes.

Within the vineyards, the outlying areas of Aisne and the Aube had been transformed. In the 1950s more than four-fifths of the Aube was planted with the Beaujolais grape Gamay, which had been used to make poor-quality fizz and that seemed to confirm the region's second-class status. Over a number of decades these were ripped out and replaced with the three champagne grapes, causing the Aube to lose the stigma of being considered the Marne's poor relation.

The surge in domestic champagne sales helped change the structure of the trade. The co-operatives expanded rapidly during the 1960s and by 1990 accounted for over half of all the growers and a third of all the vineyards in Champagne. As the co-ops merged into powerful co-operative unions, the number of family-owned merchants also began to contract. In 1963 Moët & Chandon began to acquire rivals, starting with Ruinart, the oldest House of all, followed by Mercier in 1970. Moët then merged with Hennessy, the leading Cognac House, and afterwards with the fashion company Louis Vuitton to form LVMH, which added Krug to the portfolio in 1999. The same corporate fate befell Mumm, Heidsieck Monopole, Lanson and Pommery, leaving only a handful of the old guard in family hands.

Export markets began to catch up with the surge in French sales, though progress was slow at first. Recalling his first sales trip to America in the 1960s, Pol Roger's Christian de Billy found people "had lost the habit of drinking champagne", as retold by Don Hewitson in *The Glory of Champagne*. And yet by the mid-1980s America had become champagne's biggest importer, albeit briefly. Before long the UK had wrestled the title back and by 2014 almost 33 million bottles of champagne were shipped across the Channel, with America in second place on 19 million.

A generation ago these were undreamt-of numbers for champagne. The big players had become supremely confident in their brands to the extent of setting up satellite operations like Domaine Chandon and Mumm Cuvée Napa. Yet there were always periodic crises, notably the recession of the early 1990s when sales fell and Champagne was awash with unsold stock. According to the champagne expert, Tom Stevenson, one economist even suggested the growers leave the grapes unpicked for a harvest to drain the surplus. Luckily the advice was ignored, for the world was gearing up to the biggest New Year's Eve party ever.

ABOVE Three of the best-known champagne brands, Veuve Clicquot, Moët & Chandon and Krug, are now all part of the the world's largest luxury goods maker, LVMH, Luis Vuitton Moët Hennessy.

LEFT Above the entrance to Maison Jacquart on Boulevard Lundy in Reims, there is a collection of five mosaic fresco scenes depicting the champagne-making process, including the *recoupage*.

FOLLOWING PAGES After the devastation of the First World War, Reims Cathedral was painstakingly restored with a little financial help from the Rockefellers. It finally reopened in 1938.

THE NEW MILLENNIUM

FOR ONCE, AN ERA DAWNED FULL OF HOPE AND EXPECTATION. THE ONLY BLIP ON THE RADAR WAS A PREDICTED EVENT THAT FORTUNATELY NEVER HAPPENED, AND THIS ALLOWED THE BIGGEST GLOBAL PARTY EVER TO TAKE PLACE WITHOUT A HITCH.

As the clock ticked towards midnight, 31 December 1999, there were dire warnings of a computer meltdown with planes falling from the sky. Almost worse was the prospect of no champagne. The region had been pumping up production to 270 million bottles a year since the mid-1990s and the CIVC had sanctioned the release of 132 million bottles of reserve wine. Yet still the gloomy prediction of a champagne drought days, hours, before D-day hung in the air. But in the end all was well, the internet didn't crash and the famous fizz flowed through the night.

With the morning after came the hangover, at least for those in the wine trade taken in by all the speculation and hype. In the year before, UK imports of champagne were up by one-third, while sales rose by only 19%. The supermarket Sainsbury's was said to be drowning in 800,000 surplus bottles of its own-label Blanc de Noirs. Over the Easter weekend it slashed the price to £5.99 and made a loss of £4 on every bottle, or so it was rumoured. Back in Champagne, however, it was simply a chance to replenish stocks and ride out the inevitable post-Millennial dip.

Within two or three years, sales were back at record levels and growing at over 5% annually. Despite a series of bountiful vintages as in 2004, the supply of grapes was being stretched to the limit.

"Yields are at a maximum, and we will soon have our backs to the wall," cried Moët & Chandon's then CEO, Frédéric Cumenal, in 2007. His prayers were answered that August with reports of trouble in the US subprime mortgage market. The consequences took a while to sink in, and initially there were doubts that it would spread to the so-called 'real economy'.

But spread it did, as credit lines froze and greed turned to fear in the financial markets. Global champagne sales tumbled from a 2007 all-time high of 338 million bottles to around 300 million. The age of conspicuous consumption was officially over, or at least on hold, and even the wealthiest bankers were now sipping it discreetly. But writing in his 2009 book *The Finest Wines of Champagne*, Michael Edwards wondered if: "The cold douche of market forces … may yet turn out to be a blessing in disguise for Champagne, dampening sales expectations and bringing a new mood of sober reflection to a bull market that risks losing control of prices."

As of 2015, sales had crept back to 312 million bottles, worth a record €4.75 billion. With every corner of the *appellation* planted, there has been no slack in the system for some time. After careful study, it was announced in 2008 that 40 new villages would be added to the existing 319 scattered across Champagne, and that

BELOW Grapes growing on the hilly vineyards of Philipponnat, in Mareuil-sur-Ay. They are considered to be one of the greenest of all the Champagne Houses.

BELOW LEFT The Eiffel Tower, built as temporary structure for the 1889 World's Fair but still going strong 111 years later for the great millennial celebrations.

two would be removed. The lucky ones – those growers who had been outside the magic zone for 80 years – woke up to find the value of their vineyards had shot from around €5,000 a hectare to maybe €1 million. Of course the converse was true for the two unlucky villages, whose growers immediately launched an appeal.

It is worth noting that the original champagne vineyards were once double the size of the current 33,500 hectares and that any wine from new vineyards won't be sold until the 2020s. Also, that a well-conceived revision of the *appellation* sounds far more sensible than boosting yields even further, though there are obvious concerns about prices falling through increased supply. But in volume, champagne was eclipsed by its Italian nemesis Prosecco in 2013, and today the talk is all about boosting value and justifying a higher price through better quality. An ambitious plan to improve all aspects of production, including an end to selling wine *sur latte*, was unveiled in 2012, but had yet to be ratified at the time of writing. Meanwhile some excellent bottle-fermented alternatives from across the Channel are causing a stir, at least in England.

Not all champagne is as good as it should be, but overall standards have risen, and this is perhaps most noticeable in the vineyards themselves. The race to keep up with demand has seen plantings treble since the 1950s, yet production has increased ten-fold. Powerful fertilisers and pesticides combined with more vigorous rootstocks and vines, ramped up average yields. Visitors used to report seeing vineyards sprayed by men in what looked like fall-out suits. Worse were the *bleus de ville*, or blue bags full of Parisian rubbish strewn over the ground as compost – so much for champagne's glamorous image.

But the bin bags have long gone, and since 2001 the CIVC has pledged to cut the use of chemical fertilisers, pesticides and fungicides by half. It had been shown that some of the pests were becoming immune to the sprays, while concerns over climate change were hard to ignore after the 2003 heat wave led to the earliest harvest on record. Yet in this generally cool, damp region on the edge of the winemaking world, organic vineyards are few and far between. Much more popular has been the new VDC certification (*Viticulture Durable en Champagne*), which is backed by some of the leading Houses including Bollinger and Moët & Chandon. In 2015 Caroline Henry, a sommelier and blogger who lives in Champagne, wrote in palatepress.com that she "would not be surprised if it were to become the 'greenest' wine region of France in the next few years. Quite a feat if we remember that not so long ago it was one of the most polluted regions of the country."

BELOW LEFT British TV comedy hit *Absolutely Fabulous* transferred to the big screen in 2016, with PR divas Edina Monsoon (Jennifer Saunders) and Patsy Stone (Joanna Lumley) going nowhere without bottles of Bollinger, or 'Bolly'.

BELOW Lanson has exclusively provided the champagne to serve up with the strawberries and cream at the Wimbledon Championships since 2001.

PART 3

ON THE CHAMPAGNE ROUTE

IT IS TIME TO LEAVE THE HISTORY OF THE REGION AND EXPLORE CHAMPAGNE THROUGH THE GREAT HOUSES THAT MADE IT A BYWORD FOR LUXURY AROUND THE WORLD. BEHIND THE BRANDS AND THOSE OF THE BIG CO-OPERATIVES ARE THE THOUSANDS OF GROWERS, AND BEYOND THEM THE SEA OF SPARKLING WINE MADE IN CHAMPAGNE'S IMAGE.

OPPOSITE The variety of caps matches the diversity of champagne itself, from simple and understated to colourful and charismatic, but all carefully crafted to bring pleasure to the drinker.

BILLECART-SALMON
MAREUIL-SUR-AŸ

STILL FAMILY-RUN AND FAMED FOR ITS SUBLIME, DELICATE ROSÉS, BILLECART-SALMON BELIEVE IN SUBSTANCE OVER STYLE. THIS IS RARE IN THE PR-DRIVEN WORLD OF BIG-BRAND CHAMPAGNE. "WE'RE NOT VERY FOCUSED ON MARKETING," EXPLAINS ANTOINE ROLLAND-BILLECART. "VINIFICATION IS THE KEY FOR US – THE REST IS BULLSHIT."

The animal gracing the Billecart family's seventeenth century coat of arms is not a leaping salmon, but a greyhound at full stretch beneath three bunches of grapes. The arms were authorised to Pierre Billecart by Louis XIII, and it was his descendant, Nicolas François, who founded Champagne Billecart in 1818.

The House has always been based in the pretty village of Mareuil-sur-Aÿ where Nicolas François, a local lawyer, had vineyards. To these were added six hectares of vines in the Côte des Blancs, belonging to Elisabeth Salmon's family when she married him in the 1820s. A generation or two later the families split and the old Salmon vineyards were sold off at auction in Épernay. The Billecarts tried to drop the 'S' word from the label, but the trade informed them that it was too late – their champagne was too well-known as Billecart-Salmon, and so the name stuck.

Charles Heidsieck, aka Champagne Charlie, has always taken the credit for pioneering the US market for champagne but he first crossed the Atlantic in 1852, 20 years after Billecart opened its first overseas office in New York. This nugget of family history comes from sixth-generation Antoine Rolland-Billecart, who co-runs the House with his brother François. Quite what happened to the New York office is a mystery.

Antoine believes that Billecart, like other Houses, began by producing still wine. "It was village wine like in Burgundy, and was both red and white," he says. "The bubbles came a bit later." By the 1870s Billecart-Salmon was undoubtedly sparkling and was exclusive supplier to the court of King Ludwig II of Bavaria, yet there is still a focus on what lies beneath the fizz. "We always want to remind you that champagne is a wine," says Antoine.

Billecart-Salmon was almost snuffed out by the Second World War. Mareuil-sur-Aÿ found itself caught in the conflict in 1944 between advancing American troops and Germans attempting to dig in. Antoine's father Jean had been deported to a labour camp in

TOP The founder of the dynasty – Nicolas François Billecart, the lawyer who established Champagne Billecart in 1818.

ABOVE Nicolas' wife, Elisabeth Salmon, who contributed six hectares of vineyards to the family business. Her side of the family later split and moved back to Normandy, but the name lived on.

LEFT The House's cool, damp cellars beneath the village of Mareuil-sur-Aÿ, where the secondary fermentation and bottle ageing take place.

TASTING NOTES

BILLECART-SALMON ROSÉ NV

The pretty, delicate salmon-pink hue is something of a distraction in this champagne since you are not supposed to taste its colour. It is all about restraint. It is also wonderfully fresh and pure and as clean as a whistle, but if you detect any trace of strawberry fruit, try tasting it blindfold – it may be your eyes are deceiving you.

BILLECART-SALMON CUVÉE NICOLAS FRANÇOIS BILLECART 2002

Billecart's *prestige cuvée*, is famed for its power and animal grace. It is a blend of purely Grand Cru fruit – 60% pinot noir from the Montagne and 40% chardonnay from the Côte, of which one-fifth is fermented in old oak barrels. It is intense, cerebral and elegant with the silkiest *mousse* you could imagine.

Germany for two and a half years, and when released it took him six weeks to get back from Berlin to the village. The impulse to quit the business was strong, but in 1947 he and his father began to rebuild the House slowly, focusing on the domestic market at the start. Production gradually increased from around 300,000 bottles to 2.5 million today. Exports spread slowly outwards to Belgium and Italy and reached the UK thanks to a pioneering importer: Mark Savage of Windrush Wines.

In 1954 Antoine's grandfather, Charles Rolland-Billecart, was one of the first producers to believe in rosé, which at Billecart is always referred to as 'champagne rosé' and not the other way round. The idea logic is that if blindfolded you wouldn't be able to tell its colour from the taste. Knowing how good the still red wine could be from villages like Bouzy and Mareuil, the method was always to blend it in with the white juice rather than let colour bleed in from the skins in the classic way of making a still rosé. That method may be perfect for a crisp salty Provençal rosé, but it risks adding tannin to the wine, which Billecart studiously avoid.

Either way it has become one of the most admired rosés in Champagne, though old man Billecart's neighbours thought he was "completely crazy" at the time. "Back then rosé production was not even 4% of the total," says Antoine. "Now it's above 10%." He chuckles at the memory of how some of the real grandees of champagne swore to him they would never make a pink wine. "Now of course they all do."

While his grandfather was busy in the cellar his grandmother created a beautiful garden with flowers and fruit trees around the family home in Mareuil. In 1964 they began to plant pinot noir in the parkland beyond to produce a few precious bottles of Clos Saint-Hilaire Blanc de Noirs, with a first vintage in 1995. Today this pure-bred pinot, which would have once been a still wine used for rosé, is completely biodynamic with a yield typically around half the average in Champagne.

ABOVE LEFT Some of Billecart's neatly tended vines behind the village of Mareuil-sur-Aÿ.

LEFT Billecart's cellar, where its *Sous Bois* (under oak) wines are fermented in the traditional style in large wooden vats. Sous Bois was first released in 2011.

BOLLINGER

AŸ

FIERCELY INDEPENDENT AND AS BRITISH AS JAMES BOND, BOLLINGER HAS BEEN A REMARKABLE STORY OF SURVIVAL. ESTABLISHED IN 1829, IT IS ONE OF THOSE RARE CHAMPAGNE HOUSES STILL IN FAMILY HANDS. THE FACT THAT ITS VINEYARDS SUPPLY TWO-THIRDS OF ITS NEEDS MUST BE ONE REASON WHY.

Bollinger is truly part of the Establishment thanks to its readily pronounceable name and unbroken string of royal warrants from Queen Victoria to the present day. It courses through the veins of James Bond, and it flowed through the Oxford of Evelyn Waugh, who renamed the Bullingdon Club the "Bollinger Club" in *Decline and Fall*. In more recent years "Bring out the Bolly!" became a regular Friday-night cry, whether from City traders or Sloane Rangers.

It is tempting to imagine some nineteenth-century Lord Bollinger stopping off in France on return from his Grand Tour, and founding a Champagne House to supply his friends back home. The style clearly appealed to the Brits who were drinking 85% of sales before the Second World War. In truth, however, the roots of the firm are German – not unlike those of the British Royal Family.

Born in Württemberg, Joseph Bollinger was employed as a salesman by the aristocratic de Villermont family in Aÿ along with a local, Paul-Joseph Renaudin. The family had lived there since the fifteenth century and owned 11 hectares of vineyards in Aÿ and Cuis. They decided to launch a champagne of their own, but because they did not want their name on the bottles, maybe thinking it was vulgar, the House of Renaudin-Bollinger & Cie was founded in 1829.

Athanase de Villermont was the third partner, but he died three years later. Bollinger wasted no time expanding the existing vineyards, buying a third one in Verzenay and, crucially, marrying de Villermont's daughter, Louise-Charlotte, in 1837. Renaudin died without an heir in 1854, though his name remained on the label for more than a century. Joseph Bollinger and Louis-Charlotte were left in charge and their descendants still own the business. Keeping

ABOVE A trade card for 'Bollinger's Champagne' from the 1890s, proudly displaying its royal warrants of appointment to Queen Victoria and Edward, Prince of Wales.

LEFT Bollinger's imposing headquarters in Aÿ with its façade lit up at night. The House is a pillar of the champagne establishment and a quintessential *grande marque*.

BELOW James Bond (Roger Moore) pours a glass of Bollinger for Bond girl Stacey Sutton (Tanya Roberts) in the 1985 film *A View To A Kill*.

family shareholders in check and corporate predators at bay cannot have been easy. Yet owning 165 hectares of vineyards as it does today, 85% of them grand and premier cru, must have been a useful buffer in bad times.

Either way family ownership is considered crucial, as the following lines from Bollinger's website make clear: "… No takeover by a foreign multinational, no shareholder representatives with no understanding of the vines: Bollinger is one of the last family-run houses of the Champagne region … Family, the ultimate luxury …"

In 1850 Bollinger opened a London office, which was later absorbed into the wine importers Mentzendorff. Within 40 years Mentzendorff, now owned by Bollinger, was handling almost all the sales with 89% in the UK and 7% going to the British Empire. At Victorian and Edwardian shooting parties, it was known as 'the Boy' – a reference to the young lad who would follow the guns with a pony laden with Bollinger so they could slake their thirst amidst the slaughter. Today the UK accounts for just one-tenth of the sales.

In 1911, Bollinger released its Special Cuvée (SV) for the UK, and its fulsome, rich yet dry character came to epitomise the house style. Today SV is around 60% pinot noir, 15% pinot meunier and 25% chardonnay with half the wines barrel-fermented to give a slight oakiness to the finish. SV is aged on its lees for at least three years, with typically one-tenth added from reserve wines up to 15 years old.

When Jacques Bollinger died in the Second World War, his Scottish wife Lilly was left in charge. She was another strong matriarch in the Veuve Clicquot mould who helped restore the business, and launch the innovative Bollinger RD ('recently disgorged') in 1961. As a vintage expression it showed what a decade's ageing on the lees could achieve.

Her nephew, Christian Bizot, helped broker the deal with the Bond producer Cubby Broccoli, to get Bollinger in bed with 007 [see pages 100–01] and build a very fruitful relationship. Then came the British hit television comedy *Absolutely Fabulous*, where dipsomaniac Patsy Stone (Joanna Lumley) lived on a cocktail of 'Bolly' and 'Stoli'. "The last mosquito that bit me," she once slurred, "had to check into the Betty Ford clinic." Despite concerns at Bollinger that the brand was being trashed, it seems all publicity is good publicity and sales continued to rise.

TASTING NOTES

BOLLINGER SPECIAL CUVÉE BRUT NV

Launched in 1911 and still going strong, Special Cuvée represents 90% of Bollinger's sales. Pinot noir-led with at least half fermented in oak, if offers an austere complexity on the palate that softens over time and becomes toasty with age. The palate offers lively red fruits and a sharp citrus-zest edge. It is one of the most uncompromising and complex of all standard Brut NV champagnes.

BOLLINGER GRANDE ANNÉE 2005

A hot summer with a burst of heavy rain made for a difficult growing season and the grapes tended to come in ripe, leading to wines that matured quickly. Bollinger made the best of the conditions, with a firm, well-structured wine with black cherry and tropical fruit flavours balanced by a lean, mineral finish. It is a touch drier than the Special Cuvée with a dosage of 6g/l.

ABOVE Crates of Bollinger Champagne being unloaded at Sheerness Docks in England in 1965. Before the Second World War, the British were drinking 85% of Bollinger's sales.

LEFT Madame Lilly Bollinger pedalling around the family estate. She took over the business in 1941 following the death of her husband, and played a key role in expanding and promoting the brand abroad.

DOM PÉRIGNON
HAUTVILLERS

WHENEVER THE 'DOM' IS MENTIONED IN HUSHED TONES BY WELL-HEELED *CHAMPAGNISTAS*, THEY ARE TALKING OF THE BOTTLED VERSION NOT THE FAMOUS BENEDICTINE MONK. BORN IN THE 1930s, DOM PÉRIGNON WAS LONG THE PINNACLE OF MOËT & CHANDON, BUT IN RECENT DECADES HAS DEVELOPED ITS OWN SEPARATE IDENTITY.

"Hautvillers Abbey – birthplace of champagne" declares Dom Pérignon's website in bold capitals.

"This is the place where Dom Pierre Pérignon dedicated 47 years of his life to invent and perfect the techniques to create a wine whose reputation knows no equal."

Note the word 'techniques', for he certainly did not invent champagne as we know it.

Dom Pierre Pérignon pushed the art of creation to a level of perfection never reached before in Champagne: he invented precise viticulture techniques to improve the grapes' quality; he leveraged

the art of blending with grapes coming from different crus and he introduced the gentle and fractional pressing to obtain white wines from black grapes.

The myth of Dom Pérignon, who died in 1715, was created much later. It was given a lift when Pierre-Gabriel Chandon, who had just married Adelaïde Moët, acquired the vineyards and defunct abbey of Hautvillers in the 1820s. But the big boost came in 1932. With champagne sales in the doldrums during the Depression, the Champenois decided to celebrate the 250th anniversary of the Dom's great 'invention'. It was a pretty arbitrary date, but it achieved its aim of stimulating demand.

That same year, at a meeting of the *Syndicat* of Champagne Houses, a PR man called Lawrence Venn suggested someone should launch a real luxury brand. Given the state of the global economy it sounded as daft as Marie Antoinette's famous declaration: "Let them eat cake", and the idea was quickly shot down. But it caught the attention of Robert-Jean de Voguë, who was there as Moët & Chandon's newly appointed sales director. He took Venn out to dinner and hatched a plan to create Dom Pérignon.

The champagne Dom Pérignon was launched in London in 1935, using a replica of an eighteenth-century bottle with an imposing shield for a label. It was a *Cuvée Centenaire* marking not Dom Pérignon's birthday, but the 100th anniversary of Moët & Chandon's first agency abroad, Simon Brothers. They wanted a special wine as a gift for their 100 top customers.

It was from the 1926 vintage and interestingly didn't carry the famous name. Word of its existence reached America and the following year a shipment of just 100 cases was despatched to New York aboard

ABOVE The Abbey Saint-Pierre, in Hautvillers, where Dom Pierre Pérignon was appointed cellar master in 1668. He spent almost 50 years there, perfecting the quality of his still wines.

LEFT A much photographed statue of Dom Pérignon, clutching a foaming bottle of his great 'invention', outside the headquarters of Moët & Chandon in Épernay.

TASTING NOTES

DOM PÉRIGNON 2006

While 2006 was an average vintage for most with wines not destined for longevity, DP has plenty more to give with its crisp red berry and gooseberry fruit, and fine *mousse*. Being taut on the outside yet fleshy on the inside, it will only improve with a few more years of bottle ageing.

DOM PÉRIGNON P2 1998

P2 signifies a second release of this vintage with even longer on the lees and a slightly lower *dosage*. The result will delight lovers of that bready, yeasty character of old champagne, with all the brioche and shortbread aromas you could wish for. There's marzipan and hazelnuts, yet a vibrant, lemony freshness too.

the luxury French liner, the *Normandie*. This time it was from the older, highly rated 1921 vintage, and did carry the name *Dom Pérignon*. The rest, as they say, is history.

Louis Roederer with Cristal might dispute that 'the Dom' was the first ever *prestige cuvée*, but it is the wine that other Houses have sought to copy. Unlike Krug's *Grande Cuvée* or Taittinger's *Comtes de Champagne*, however, it has always been a vintage wine. How much is produced today is a closely guarded secret, and estimates vary wildly from 3.5–8 million bottles. It is almost entirely sourced from Moët's own vineyards with a roughly equal blend of chardonnay from grand cru villages like Avize and Cramant, and pinot noir from the best sites in Aÿ, Ambonay, Bouzy and the like. In all some 21 villages contribute.

In 1971, it was joined by a rosé whose first vintage was 1959. Among the first to enjoy it were world leaders who joined the Shah of Iran to celebrate the 2,500th anniversary of the Persian Empire. The party in Persepolis reputedly cost over US$100 million. Today Dom Pérignon Rosé accounts for a fraction of total sales, and usually costs at least double the main expression.

Initially Dom Pérignon was released in roughly two out of every five vintages, but since 1997 only the 2001 was not released. Richard Geoffroy, Dom Pérignon's long-standing *chef de cave*, has said he wants to make it every year, albeit in much reduced quantities in difficult years. Interpreting the unique character of the seasons involves elements of risk; it is a commitment to renewed creation, a reinvention every year. In *The Champagne Guide* by Tyson Stelzer, he said: "I'm often asked about global warming and I am embarrassed to say that so far it has been for the better in Champagne."

ABOVE Estimates of the wine's annual production vary wildly from 3.5 million to 8 million bottles, but the true figure remains a closely guarded secret.

LEFT Richard Geoffroy, Dom Pérignon's highly regarded *chef de cave*, wants to produce Dom Pérignon Rosé every year if possible.

FOLLOWING PAGES Panoramic shot of the Dom Perignon vinyards, the town of Hautvillers and the surrounding lands.

GOSSET
AŸ

GOSSET HAS BEEN MAKING WINE IN THE VILLAGE OF AŸ SINCE THE SIXTEENTH CENTURY. UNTIL THE ADVENT OF STRONG GLASS BOTTLES MADE OF ENGLISH GLASS ONE ASSUMES IT WAS ALL STILL WINE. YET, MORE THAN 430 YEARS LATER, THIS FINE BOUTIQUE *MAISON* IS STILL GOING STRONG UNDER ITS NEW OWNERSHIP.

Dom Pérignon was not even a twinkle in his grandmother's eye when Pierre Gosset set up his wine business in the village of Aÿ in 1584. It was just down the road from the Dom's abbey and at the time much more famous for its wines than Hautvillers. Consider that Francis I of France and Henry VIII of England both kept cellars in the village. Indeed Francis decreed he was not just king of France, but also *Roi d'Aÿ et de Gonesse* (King of Aÿ and Gonesse – the latter being a town famed for its flour).

So why then let Ruinart bask in the glory of being 'the first Champagne House', founded 145 years later in 1729? Well, it all comes down to a question of definition. Gosset claims only to be the first 'Wine House', and until some evidence is unearthed of an early departure into bottles that sparkled, one has to assume its production was entirely of still wine. Not that Ruinart can prove it was producing fizz from day one, but according to the current MD, Jean-Pierre Cointreau: "there's a very precise agreement between the two Houses". It is clearly one they both respect.

As with just about every Champagne House before the early nineteenth century, no one bothered to document the moment of transition from still to sparkling champagne, or if they did the records have long disappeared. What is remarkable about the Gosset family, given the Napoleonic Code of subdividing inheritance between siblings, is that the last Gosset was still running the business as late as 1994.

This was Etienne Gosset, whose father had used his fortune from the sale of the Rochas perfume company, where he was a key partner, to buy control of the House. However, given there had been sixteen generations since Pierre Gosset, the vineyard holdings had been scattered between a veritable army of cousins. By the mid-1980s the House owned just 10 hectares, having made a killing selling off some prime sites to Krug the previous decade, while production was a modest 250,000 bottles.

When Gosset was sold to its present owners – Groupe Renauld Cointreau – in 1994, it came with just a hectare of vines. "Of course financially speaking you are better off owning vineyards," says Jean-Pierre Cointreau. "However, champagne is a blend of different wines from different areas, and we work with 140 growers, some who have been supplying Gosset for three generations. So the

ABOVE The 'oldest Wine House in Champagne', dating back to 1584, is not quite the same as 'the oldest Champagne House' – that title is held by Ruinart, founded 145 years later.

LEFT Gosset's offices in Aÿ, where François I of France and Henry VIII of England kept wine cellars. Both kings died in 1547, and 37 years later Pierre Gosset started his family wine business in the village.

advantage of not having vineyards is that it gives you this diversity and you can really create the blend as you wish."

The Cointreau family own Frapin Cognac, and though they came as outsiders to Champagne, there was one vital thread of continuity from the days of Etienne Gosset. That thread was the late *chef de cave*, Jean-Pierre Mareigner, a true local from Aÿ, who spent almost his entire career at Gosset, having joined in 1983, aged 27. His father had been vineyard director beforehand. By all accounts Mareigner was on close, first-name terms with all the growers. "He knew how to select the best grapes, the best juice and he knew the people who grew the best grapes," said the firm's former UK importer, Peter McKinley, at the time of Mareigner's death in 2016. "The seriously sad thing for Gosset Champagne is that Jean-Pierre was the family memory, the company memory."

He will be a hard act to follow, but it seems he was planning to retire in 2017 and had amassed a great team around him. Gosset is still very much a boutique Champagne House, though annual production has increased to around 1.1 million bottles. Since 2009, there has been plenty of scope for future growth since buying from Laurent-Perrier an impressive winery and cellar in Épernay next door to Pol Roger.

As a result Gosset is now blessed with the luxury of space and can give its top wines as much ageing on the lees as it wishes. Some 40% of its production is its highly rated Grande Reserve which, like all Gosset wines, are bottled in a bulbous, slender-necked copy of an eighteenth-century bottle.

TASTING NOTES

GOSSET GRANDE RÉSERVE BRUT NV

While there is a more entry-level "Brut Excellence", it's really worth stretching to the much-admired Grande Réserve. All Champagne Houses boast of elegance and finesse, but this wine has it in spades along with a whiff of spice and the faintest trace of digestive biscuits through bottle age.

GOSSET GRAND MILLÉSIME 2006

Grapes were picked healthy and ripe, but with relatively low acidity such that this wine was drinking beautifully as of 2016. It has a delightfully creamy, soft texture to balance the vibrant, crisp fruit with notes of lemon zest, green apples and a firm, dried spice finish.

ABOVE The bulbous thin-necked bottles used for champagne in the 18th century have been faithfully copied for Gosset.

LEFT The House currently produces around 1.1 million bottles a year, 40% of which is its highly rated Grande Reserve.

BELOW Pierre Gosset, alderman of Aÿ, founded the company in 1584, but Gosset did not produce champagne until the 18th century.

HENRIOT
REIMS

HENRIOT'S FOUNDER, APOLLINE GODINOT, WAS A CLASSIC CHAMPAGNE WIDOW IN THE MOULD OF HER EARLY NINETEENTH CENTURY CONTEMPORARY, BARBE NICOLE CLICQUOT PONSARDIN. IF HENRIOT IS NOT QUITE AS FAMOUS AS VEUVE CLICQUOT, IT IS STILL IN FAMILY HANDS AND GAINING IN REPUTATION UNDER ITS DYNAMIC *CHEF DE CAVES*.

In 1794 Apolline married Nicolas Henriot, from a long line of drapers in Reims, and brought with her some vineyards in the Montagne de Reims. With this dowry and on her husband's death in 1808, she founded the house Veuve Henriot Ainé. Henriot has been family-run ever since, though Appoline's grandson Ernest Henriot took time out to help his cousin Charles Heidsieck with his champagne house in 1851. He stayed there until 1875, when he returned to look after Henriot, which was already supplying the Dutch Court, and went on to supply the Hapsburg dynasty in its twilight years. The bond between the houses of Henriot and Heidsieck was finally cemented by Joseph Henriot, who bought Charles Heidsieck a century later, only to sell it to Rémy Martin in 1985.

Joseph Henriot was a consummate deal-maker, and not just in Champagne. Having absorbed Heidsieck, he proceeded to sell almost the entire Henriot estate to LVMH. The luxury goods giant gained 125 hectares, including a swathe of valuable vineyards in the Côtes des Blancs in return for an 11% share in Veuve Clicquot. As the largest individual share-holder, Joseph became the boss and is credited with building Veuve Clicquot into a global brand before leaving LVMH in 1994 to turn his attention to restoring the somewhat neglected house of Henriot.

A year later he expanded his wine empire into Burgundy, buying the *négociant*, Bouchard Père et Fils, followed by William Fevre in Chablis, leaving his son Stanislas to run the champagne business in 1999. Joseph died in 2015, and today Maisons & Domaine Henriot

ABOVE Like any self-respecting *Maison de Champagne*, Henriot marks its vineyards in stone..

LEFT 18 metres beneath the streets of Reims, Henriot's cellars boast a cool, constant 11C.

TASTING NOTES

HENRIOT NV BLANC DE BLANCS

Made primarily from Côtes des Blanc fruit, this is a crisp, lively lemon-scented wine with a feint trace of white flowers, possibly honeysuckle, as well. It has more depth and texture than many a Blanc de Blancs.

HENRIOT CUVÉE HEMERA 2005

Henriot's new top *cuvée* is an equal blend of chardonnay and pinot noir from six grand cru villages in the Côtes des Blancs and the Montagne de Reims. After eight years on the lees, it is nutty, honeyed, sumptuous – almost decadent – and has a bright citric edge.

is chaired by his nephew, Gilles de Larouzière. Since that deal with LVMH, Henriot has lost all its *Grand Cru* holdings in the Côtes des Blancs and now owns just 35 hectares in all. These include 12 in Chouilly – Grand Cru for Chardonnay – and 11 in Aÿ, Mareuil-sur-Aÿ and Avenay.

Despite all the changes at the top, and the focus on building Henriot's export markets, the wines themselves have not been neglected thanks in large part to the talents of Henriot's highly-regarded cellar master, Laurent Fresnet. The son of a local grower, with wine-making experience in the New World, Fresnet wanted to sharpen up the house style when he took on the role in 2006. "What we changed was to be much more mineral, more fruity and more elegant," he says.

By 2010 the results were beginning to show through in Henriot NV, which represents 95% of the 1.5 million bottles produced. This is particularly true of the flagship Blanc de Blancs which is carefully constructed each year. Some 70% of the grapes are bought from outside, from growers whose plots express a specific terroir. Collectively, they form a spice rack for Fresnet to work his magic, like a chef in the kitchen. "I don't blend wine, I blend fruit," he explains. "It starts from the vineyards in the summertime, tasting the berries and trying to find some balance between the villages."

Yet what sets Henriot apart in his view, is its treasure chest of reserve wines that are used to fine tune the base wines from a particular year. These are kept in separate stainless steel tanks according to vineyard and vintage. Justifying the expense of this painstaking approach might not be easy in a big, corporate champagne house, but Henriot has the luxury of being family-owned. Fresnet insists that no-one in accounts has ever imposed a budget on what he spends every year to secure the best grapes going.

Above the standard Brut Souverain NV – a 50:50 blend of Chardonnay and Pinot Noir, and various vintage expressions, including Hemera – is Henriot's famous Cuve 38, that Joseph Henriot launched in 1990. It is based on the Grand Cru villages of Oger, Mesnil-sur-Oger, Chouilly and Avize in the Côtes des Blancs. The wines are vatted together in a giant stainless steel tank that holds 467 hectolitres. Every year 15% of the blend is refreshed with new wine and 15% is drawn off as a reserve wine, some of which is bottled as Cuve 38 that boasts an average age of 18 years.

ABOVE Ripening chardonnay vines destined for Henriot's Brut Souverain NV.

LEFT Laurent Fresnet, Henriot's highly rated *chef de caves*.

JACQUESSON

DIZY

DESPITE ITS LATE EIGHTEENTH CENTURY ROOTS, JACQUESSON HAS REINVENTED ITSELF IN THE MOULD OF A MODERN CHAMPAGNE GROWER THANKS TO THE CHIQUET BROTHERS WHO HAVE TRIMMED BACK SALES IN PURSUIT OF QUALITY. THEIR MAVERICK APPROACH STANDS OUT FROM THE CORPORATE WORLD OF "BIG CHAMPAGNE" DRIVEN BY THE NEED TO GROW BRANDS.

Jean-Hervé Chiquet describes the firm bought by his father in 1978, as: "a classic little champagne house that my brother and I transformed over 30 years into a grower-like operation." He and Laurent Chiquet took over in 1988, which is when everything began to change. "There is no continuity between Jacquesson of the past and Jacquesson now," Jean-Hervé says.

For all that, the house was established in 1798 in what is now Châlons-en-Champagne by Memmie Jacquesson and found an early admirer in Napoleon. Sales took off under Memmie's son Adolphe, and exports had reached the USA by 1849, the year Tom Stevenson recalls is his *World Encyclopedia of Champagne and Sparkling Wine* that a shipment was abandoned in San Francisco Bay when the entire crew deserted to join the gold rush. Bottles unearthed from the mud 30 years later were said to have had "a very fair flavour" having "effervesced slightly on uncorking".

From a peak of selling more than a million bottles in 1867, Jacquesson went downhill, and by the time it was acquired in 1978 sales were around 450,000 from some 45 hectares of vineyards, of which one-third were owned by the house. Operations were shifted to the village of Dizy, west of Aÿ and, after 14 years, old man Chiquet handed over the reins to his sons. He was, according to Jean-Hervé: "fed up with two guys saying the same thing every morning."

"We found that to make good wine you need three things; good terroir, but that's just pure luck to be born in the right place. You need to work hard, that's obvious, but third and very important; you mustn't keep what's not good enough." The result is that: "Today the *domaine* has grown to 29 hectares, but buying contracts have gone from 30 to 8 hectares and production has dropped to 250,000 bottles," he explains. "If you tell me that it's an unusual

BELOW LEFT Jean-Hervé Chiquet (left) and his brother Laurent.

BELOW The Chiquets like to ferment their wines in oak to add oxygen rather than flavour.

TASTING NOTES

CHAMPAGNE JACQUESSON *CUVÉE NO. 741* EXTRA BRUT

Based on the 2013 vintage, *Cuvée 741* is a blend of just over half chardonnay, and an equal split of pinot noir and pinot meunier. A fifth is reserve wine which helps to balance the generous citrus, gooseberry and apple fruit, and round off the firm, dry finish.

JACQUESSON *CUVÉE 737 DEGORGEMENT TARDIF*

After seven and a half years on the lees, the fruit from what is mainly the 2009 vintage has evolved an earthy, bruised apple and lemon zest character to compliment the elegant, mineral-flecked acidity underneath. The combination works brilliantly.

business model, you're right!"

Jean-Hervé goes on to say: "There's something not quite right in producing only 250,000 bottles from 37 hectares." It equates to about 70% of what a typical champagne house would produce, thanks partly to lower yields in the vineyard and partly to a refusal to use the second pressing, or *taille*. The Chiquets have gradually gone organic, entering what Jean-Hervé calls: "a sort of virtuous circle" with less vigorous vines being more resistant to disease. Not that it's easy to go green in Champagne where the biggest problem is mildew, especially in years like 2012.

The vineyards lie in the Vallée de la Marne and the Côtes des Blancs, half planted with Chardonnay, 30% Pinot Noir and the rest an ever-declining proportion of Pinot Meunier. Fermentation is carried out in wooden vats to help oxygenate the wine during vinification rather than add oaky flavours to the end result. But what really sets Jacquesson apart is the absence of a house style. This is because the Chiquets see themselves as growers rather than proprietors of a champagne house, and because they don't want to be constrained by some self-imposed style. "For us the idea of making the same wine every year would be extremely boring," says Jean-Hervé.

This philosophy gave birth to the brothers' one and only blend that started with *Cuvée 700*. The idea is simply to try and create the best blend possible each year using reserve wines to add complexity rather than achieve consistency. In 2005, with *Cuvée 733* they decided to hold back some of the wine and release it much later as a *dégorgement tardif* (late disgorged) bottling. This is something they

have done every year since, allowing Jacquesson fans to compare two versions of the same blend, one with around four years' ageing on the lees, the other with around nine. They do make other champagnes including a vintage, but the focus is very much on the *Cuvée* which represents an antidote to Non-Vintage conformity. "Our approach is essentially selfish," says Jean-Hervé, who goes on to explain his target audience: "Basically we make the wine for the two best customers of Jacquesson – Laurent and I."

ABOVE After the first pressing in a traditional vertical press, the second pressing or *taille* is sold on.

LEFT Long ageing on the lees helps imbue Jacquesson with its finesse and complexity.

JOSEPH PERRIER
CHÂLONS-EN-CHAMPAGNE

STILL FAMILY-OWNED, AND ONE OF THE ORIGINAL *GRANDES MARQUES*, JOSEPH PERRIER HAS BEEN REFERRED TO AS 'THE OTHER PERRIER' – APPARENTLY IT'S NOT AN UNCOMMON NAME IN THESE PARTS. AS THE ONLY LEADING CHAMPAGNE HOUSE IN CHÂLONS-EN-CHAMPAGNE, IT SITS WELL TO THE SOUTH-EAST OF THE MAIN ACTION AROUND REIMS AND ÉPERNAY.

The firm's roots go back to Perrier Fils, who were wine merchants in what was then Châlons-sur-Marne at the start of the nineteenth century. One branch of the family moved to Éperna,y where Pierre-Nicolas-Marie Perrier-Jouët established his House. Fourteen years later in 1825, his nephew Joseph Perrier set up in Châlons, then a key champagne town with 13 Houses of good repute. Today it is the sole survivor.

In the 1880s Joseph's grandson, Gabriel Perrier, sold out to Paul Pithois, another local wine merchant, whose great-grandson Jean-Claude Fourmon now runs the business. The name never changed because Joseph Perrier was well established in France and the West Indies, and was also in India and the UK by the time of its sale. A decade later the new owners could count Queen Victoria and Edward Prince of Wales among their customers. The *dosage* levels were apparently very sweet.

Pithois had a holiday home in the village of Cumières on the banks of the Marne, where he acquired nine hectares of vineyards, and in neighbouring Hautvillers and Daméry, which the family still own. He was also the first secretary of the Syndicat du Marques du Champagne, and was involved with the great French scientist, Louis Pasteur.

Châlons was largely unscathed by the First World War, and the firm was happy to help the Krug family store their wine in its cellars while the German artillery pulverised Reims. Joseph Perrier survived the lean, inter-war years and the wave of buy-ups after the war. "During the 1960s the Marne valley developed from fruit farming to vineyards," says Jean-Claude Fourmon, whose uncles bought more south-facing vineyards around Verneuil along the Marne to swell the family's holdings to 21 hectares. Another uncle, a dashing colonel in the French army, who spoke impeccable English, helped develop the UK market.

The vineyards lean towards pinot noir and pinot meunier, though the core wine, the Cuvée Royal NV Brut, includes an equal share of chardonnay in the blend. It comes with a distinctive pale lemon-yellow label in contrast to the egg-yolk colours of Veuve Clicquot, and accounts for at least three-quarters of sales. Above sits the Vintage Brut Cuvée and Cuvée Josephine, a majestic 60:40 marriage of chardonnay and pinot noir.

The decision of whether to declare a vintage starts with "the quality of the grapes when they're picked", says Fourmon. "We look at the balance between acidity and the potential alcohol in the juice. The second step is when we have the juice vinified before blending, when we can assess the quality in the *vin clair* from the different villages from our own grapes and what we buy in. Then we look at the wine just before bottling and see what the other *chefs de caves* are doing."

LEFT One of the estate-owned vineyards on the road to Hautvillers. It was here and in neighbouring Daméry and Cumières that Paul Pithois acquired nine hectares in the 1880s.

BELOW An autumnal view of some of Joseph Perrier's vineyards on the banks of the river Marne, near the Premier Cru village of Cumières.

TASTING NOTES

JOSEPH PERRIER CUVÉE ROYALE BRUT NV

The other 'yellow label' to Veuve Clicquot's, Cuvée Royale is an ethereal, light, classic apéritif-style champagne made from an equal blend of the three grapes sourced from 20 villages including Cumières, Damery and Hautvillers. There's a whiff of pear on the nose, a supple texture and a lively, fresh finish.

JOSEPH PERRIER CUVÉE JOSEPHINE 2004

JP's top *cuvée* "can be a wonderful expression of ripe, mature chardonnay," wrote Michael Edwards in *The Finest Wines of Champagne*, and the 2004 is no exception. Rich, almost buttery in texture, but with clean, bright lemony fruit and with a near perfect poise and balance.

Once the grapes are crushed in presses near the vineyards, the juice is transported to Châlons, a good half an hour away. The winery is an old townhouse and boasts some spectacular Gallo-Roman cellars cut horizontally into the side of a small hill some 2,000 years ago. They were extended to three kilometres in the mid-nineteenth century, when shafts were sunk into the hillside for ventilation and natural light.

Like many Houses, Joseph Perrier went through tough times in the mid-1990s after the First Gulf War and the surge in oil prices. It was unable to recapitalise the business, and Laurent-Perrier acquired a majority share until it too was in trouble. With the two names so close it was unclear how the smaller Perrier would fit it, but luckily Fourmon's first cousin Alain Thiénot came to the rescue. With his own champagne brand, to which he has since added Canard-Duchêne, he was able to buy out Laurent-Perrier in 1998. Joseph Perrier has thus slipped back into that select band of family-owned Houses like Pol Roger and Roederer.

A few years later the town of Châlons managed to swap its suffix from 'sur-Marne' to 'en-Champagne', much to Fourmon's delight. "That made Épernay and Reims so jealous!" he says with barely suppressed glee. "Now we can have 'champagne' twice on our labels."

ABOVE LEFT The original Gallo-Roman cellars in Châlons-en-Champagne were extended three kilometres in the nineteenth century.

FAR LEFT An Art Deco poster for the brand from the 1920s by J Stall (1874–1933).

LEFT Item of correspondence between the office of the Prince of Wales (later King Edward VII) and Joseph Perrier, which was to buy 100 bottles of champagne. The Prince had sampled the 1884 vintage and placed the order for the 1890 vintage 15 months in advance.

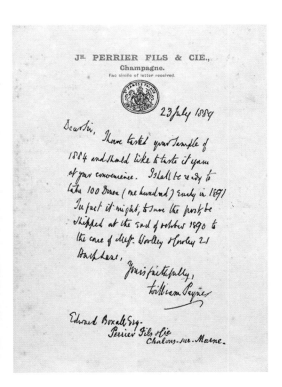

KRUG

REIMS

WHETHER KRUG IS THE WORLD'S GREATEST CHAMPAGNE IS OBVIOUSLY A MATTER OF OPINION, BUT IT IS CLEARLY WHAT THE *CHEF DE CAVE*, ERIC LEBEL, AND HIS TEAM AIM FOR EACH YEAR WHEN THEY RELEASE KRUG GRANDE CUVÉE. THE ATTENTION TO DETAIL IS AWESOME, AS IS THE PRICE.

"With Krug there is no hierarchy," says sixth-generation director Olivier Krug, and by that he means the multi-vintage Grande Cuvée is made to be the equal of vintage Krug with as much care taken in its production. Also, unlike other houses, there is no cheaper NV version to give a glimpse of greatness. Priced at around £130 a bottle, Grande Cuvée occupies a rarefied niche and there's not much of it. Krug's total production is less than 0.2% of champagne, which puts it below 625,000 bottles a year.

The story starts in 1834, when Joseph Krug, an ambitious young German, began working for the leading house at the time: Champagne Jacquesson in Châlons-sur-Marne. Before long he was co-managing the business and married to his partner's English sister-in-law, Emma Anne Jaunay. Instead of cruising into a comfortable retirement, he departed to set up his own business in Reims in 1843. He had the backing of a local wine merchant, for whom he had been blending wine on the side.

The art of blending was the key to quality, in his view, a vision he expressed in a small red notebook in 1848. "Joseph wrote that if you want to make a great wine you need good elements from good origins," says Olivier. The latter referred to the *terroir*, while the 'elements' were the base wines that made up the blend. Some would have been produced years earlier and held back as reserve wines, which gave him the means to circumvent the vagaries of a particular vintage and produce a top champagne every year.

He died in 1866: his son Paul took over. The wine was already selling as far afield as St Petersburg, New York and Rio de Janeiro, and being half-English, Paul helped to establish the champagne across the Channel. In the 1880s Paul Krug bought the first vineyards – 20 hectares around Mailly on the Montagne de Reims, but then sold them to focus on what he felt the family did best: blending. While the name 'Grande Cuvée' is more recent, the wine has stayed true to the founder's original vision.

Today the cuvee is a blend of wines from different years stretching back 15 years, with the youngest component never less than five, and first fermented in oak barrels. With up to a further

ABOVE RIGHT After nine years of honing his craft with Champagne Jacquesson in Châlons-sur-Marne, Johann-Josef Krug, founded a House of his own in 1843.

ABOVE The founder's leather-bound journal in which he recorded his notes and observations on the art of blending champagne.

RIGHT Olivier Krug, descendant of Joseph Krug, at work on his cuvées. His father, Henri, likened the blending process to "the creation of a symphony".

year's ageing after disgorgement, the wine's greatest ingredient may well be time. While the company's greatest asset is its unrivalled collection of reserve wines and the skill of Eric Lebel to marry them in the best possible way. The specific composition of every bottle can be discovered using the Krug ID; six digits on the back of the bottle.

The fifth generation, Henri Krug, who died in 2013, was fond of musical metaphors. He described blending as: "the creation of a symphony … in an orchestra each musical instrument is essential, from the violins and cellos to the flutes, oboes, bassoons, etc. Each one of them playing its part and contributing to the harmony of the whole work."

Olivier Krug is keen to dispel perceptions that his champagne is just for the elite, or connoisseurs. "Krug is about spontaneity and generosity, it's not about excluding people. When I read what's been written that 'there is champagne, and there is Krug' or that 'Krug starts where others stop' I think, 'What arrogance!' That's really not what Krug's about." To make the point he quotes a tweet from Madonna. "She was asked if she had a guilty pleasure, and she immediately tweeted back: 'French fries and Krug Rosé champagne'."

In the early 1970s Krug finally acquired vineyards of its own, including Clos du Mesnil, a tiny walled vineyard of 1.9 hectares in the village of Mesnil-sur-Oger that was originally planted by Benedictine monks at the end of the seventeenth century. The purchase of what has become arguably the greatest single vineyard champagne of all involved a partnership with the cognac house Rémy Martin, which in turn led to Krug's sale to LVMH in 1999. Some say Krug slightly lost its way until Maggie Henriquez, a dynamic Venezuelan, took charge in 2009. Today it glitters as bright as ever.

TASTING NOTES

KRUG GRANDE CUVÉE BRUT NV

Krug's pride and joy is a moveable feast of grape varieties from up to 200 carefully selected plots, with reserve wines accounting for up to half the blend. The result is a firm, rich, golden champagne with some mellow dried fruits at its core, a fine *mousse* and a toasty, nutty aroma.

KRUG 2003 BRUT

It must have been challenging in the extreme to make a vintage wine after the 2003 heat wave led to the earliest harvest since 1822, but Krug pulled it off. It is a testament to the wizardry of winemaker Eric Lebel who blended this golden-hued beauty with its brioche-like aromas and citrus, red-fruit core.

ABOVE LEFT A grand old bottle of Krug with its imperial crest. Note the word *Sec,* signifying a *dosage* of more than 17 grams/litre of sugar which, by today's standards, would be anything but 'dry'.

LEFT A prime piece of Champagne real estate – the fabled walled vineyard of Clos du Mesnil in the village of Mesnil-sur-Oger, which Krug acquired in the early 1970s.

LANSON
REIMS

THERE WAS CERTAINLY AN ELEMENT OF TRAGEDY IN THE RISE AND FALL OF THE GREAT MAISON LANSON DURING THE 1990s. BUT SINCE 2006 IT HAS BEEN UNDER NEW OWNERSHIP AS PART OF THE INDEPENDENT LANSON-BCC GROUP, AND IS DETERMINED TO TAKE ON MOËT & CHANDON AND VEUVE CLICQUOT AND WIN.

It began with a marriage between François Delamotte of Reims, who owned a fairly sizeable vineyard in Cumières in the Marne valley, and Marie-Claude Thérèse de Bourgogne, whose father had a vineyard in Aÿ. The combined holding encouraged François to set up his own Champagne House in 1760. Some 40 years later, his youngest son, Nicolas-Louis, took over and, as a newly decorated Knight of the Order of Malta, decided to use the famous Maltese cross as the emblem of his champagne.

The Lansons didn't arrive on the scene until 1837, when Jean-Baptiste Lanson, an old friend of the family, became a director and eventually succeeded as sole owner of the firm. It changed its name to Lanson Père & Fils and under Jean-Baptiste's son, Victor-Marie Lanson, sales began to take off, especially in the UK where it was distributed by the well-established London merchants Percy Fox. In 1900 it won a converted new customer in Queen Victoria, and has held a royal warrant ever since.

Lanson's real growth began in the late 1920s, when it acquired some superb cellars and land on the Rue de Courlancy in the heart of Reims. In charge was the formidable figure of Victor Lanson, who travelled widely selling to everyone from Indian maharajas to gold miners who had struck it rich in Australia. Meanwhile back in Champagne he began seriously to expand the family's vineyards, which eventually reached 208 hectares.

Victor Lanson was one of the first big merchants to develop a rosé champagne, and to buy pinot noir from the Aube. This was the key grape in the firm's flagship Lanson Black Label NV Brut that first appeared in 1938. Whether he was inspired by a certain Johnnie Walker, the name has always been in English, even in France. "I only make champagne for myself. What I can't drink I sell," was one of Victor's catchphrases, and as a man who averaged three bottles a day, or so it was claimed, it wasn't such an idle boast.

As the Lanson family grew, it became more complicated to manage with 17 private shareholders, a number of outside investors and the potential for lots of infighting. During the 1970s the Gardinière family, in-laws of the Lansons who had made a fortune flogging fertilisers in America, steadily acquired all the shares. In 1984 they sold out to the BSN group, with sixth-generation Jean-Baptiste Lanson still in charge. He insisted it was better for the champagne to be part of a large, professional group than a vast, squabbling family, but things took a turn for the worst.

Thanks to Black Label, Lanson was selling up to 10 million bottles a year and was second only to Moët & Chandon when the First Gulf War kicked off in August 1990. The subsequent oil crisis caused the champagne market to crash and Moët seized its chance and pounced the following year. It wasn't interested in the brand,

ABOVE In the heart of Reims, with the city's cathedral in the background, pickers set to work on the one-hectare walled vineyard of Clos Lanson. In 2016, Lanson announced it would be using the grapes to produce a single vineyard cuvée.

LEFT Clos Lanson is a Blanc de Blancs, fermented in oak barrels and left on its lees for eight years. On average, only 8,000 bottles will be produced.

or the company's headquarters in Reims, so much as those lovely vineyards. This became clear when Lanson was quickly sold to the giant Marne et Champagne group, who acquired the brand, the company HQ, the cellars and four years of stocks, but not a single vine. Astonishingly they paid the same amount for which it had been sold six months earlier.

Given the eye-watering prices of a good vineyard nowadays, it was an astonishingly good deal for the owners of Moët & Chandon, who almost crippled their closest rival in the process. "When an important champagne house loses its vital vineyards," wrote Michael

Edwards in *The Finest Wines of Champagne*, "any candid *chef de cave* will tell you that it takes a good fifteen years to re-establish the best sort of contracted grape suppliers and build up reserve wines in the quest for top quality."

All the while Lanson has been a long-term sponsor of Wimbledon, where some 25,000 bottles of Black Label, at around £70 a pop, are sold during the fortnight, though the weather and Andy Murray's fortunes play a big part in determining sales. Maybe an English sparkler is plotting to replace it, but for now Lanson appears safe.

TASTING NOTES

LANSON BLACK LABEL BRUT NV

Black Label may have been a bit too much of a crowd-pleaser in the past with its faults smothered under a high *dosage*, but it is a lot more elegant these days. With a blend that is one-half pinot noir and one-third chardonnay, there is a core of red fruit and lemon syllabub on the tongue and a muted aroma of spring flowers.

LANSON MILLÉSIME GOLD LABEL 2005

Chef de cave Hervé Danton and his team delight in producing opulent, toasty vintage champagnes. The 2005 is a roughly equal marriage of pinot noir and chardonnay entirely from *grands crus* villages. It has a honeyed, crusty bread aroma, a fleshy texture and a firm structure with a chalky, mineral edge.

TOP LEFT A classic pupitre in the Lanson cellar.

TOP MIDDLE Some 25,000 bottles of Lanson champagne are sold at the Wimbledon tennis championships each year, at around £70 a pop. Sales are very much weather- and Andy Murray-dependent.

LEFT Hervé Dantan, *chef de cave* at Lanson, studies the depth of colour and assesses the aroma before tasting the wine in the cellars.

LAURENT-PERRIER

TOURS-SUR-MARNE

NOW INTO ITS THIRD CENTURY, LAURENT-PERRIER WAS A VERY SMALL BRAND BEFORE THE SECOND WORLD WAR. ITS RENAISSANCE SINCE THEN TO BECOME ONE OF THE BIG BEASTS OF CHAMPAGNE WAS DOWN TO ONE MAN ABOVE ALL: THE LEGENDARY BERNARD DE NONANCOURT, WHO DIED AGED 90 IN 2010.

On 4 May 1945, de Nonancourt, then a young tank commander, found himself in the Bavarian Alps beneath Hitler's secret mountain hideaway the Eagle's Nest – as recalled in *Wine & War*, by Don and Petie Kladstrup. Because he was from Champagne and knew something about wine, he was ordered to investigate a cave beneath the summit, believed to contain the Führer's personal cellar. Having dynamited the steel door, de Nonancourt squeezed in to discover an incredible stash of wine. Amidst the Châteaux Lafite, Margaux and d'Yquem were hundreds of cases of Salon. He could not have imagined that, albeit 44 years later, he would add this glittering boutique brand to his champagne empire.

Founded in 1812 in Tours-sur-Marne by André-Michel Pierlot, the House was named after the cellar master Eugène Laurent, who inherited the business only to die accidentally in 1887, leaving his wife in charge. Mathilde Emilie Perrier was another of those redoubtable champagne widows who began to build what was now Laurent-Perrier. She pioneered a *sans-sucre* version for the UK market with the strapline: "The champagne recommended when others are prohibited." It was resurrected as Laurent-Perrier Ultra Brut in 1981.

BELOW "Never drink water" declares this cheeky statue at Laurent-Perrier but, with its cellars full to the brim with champagne, there is a tempting alternative within reach.

On the eve of the First World War, Laurent-Perrier's cellars held a respectable 600,000 bottles. By 1939, after the devastation of the war and the Depression, that number had shrunk to just 36,000. Its new owner, Marie-Louise Lanson de Nonancourt, bricked up the cellar, installed a statue of the Virgin Mary and waited for her sons to return. The eldest, Maurice, died in a concentration camp, so it was left to Bernard to rebuild Laurent-Perrier.

His mother insisted he had a thorough apprenticeship in all aspects of production at her family's Champagne House, Lanson, until she was satisfied he was serious. In 1948 he took over a business with 20 staff and sales of 80,000 bottles a year. With his cellar master Edouard Leclerc and then Alain Terrier, he developed the fresh, elegant house style with chardonnay accounting for half the NV Brut, and the use of a special strain of yeast to enhance the fruit over any bread-like aromas. The House was a pioneer in using temperature-controlled stainless-steel fermentation tanks.

Another early innovation was a rosé in 1968, when the colour pink was considered frivolous in the extreme by any serious Champagne House. The method chosen was that of a still wine like a Provençal rosé, where the colour bleeds in from the skins of black grapes, in this case pinot noir, and not by blending in a drop of red wine.

"Our belief is that you'll get the fruit on the nose and palate right

LEFT With only 110 hectares in Champagne, Laurent-Perrier is hardly self-sufficient in grapes. But Bernard de Nonancourt always maintained it was better to have contracts with good growers than own poor vineyards.

BELOW LEFT The former World War 2 tank commander Bernard de Nonancourt, in the grounds of the famous Champagne House he built up after joining the firm in 1948.

BELOW Launched in the early 1980s, Ultra Brut was inspired by the success of the *Zéro Dosage* champagnes produced by Laurent-Perrier in the late nineteenth century.

the way through to the finish," explains David Hesketh, head of Laurent-Perrier UK. "For us it's not the colour that matters, because that varies from one *cuvée* to the next."

The House owns just 110 hectares, about one-tenth of its needs, but as Hesketh explains: "De Nonancourt's philosophy was that it's better to have contracts with good growers, than to own poor vineyards." He believed the real secret was in the blend and this was exemplified by Grand Siècle, first released in 1959 as a marriage of the '52, '53 and '55 vintage. Bottled in a replica champagne bottle from Versailles at the time of Louis XIV, the Sun King, it has always been a trio of top years, apart from twice when it was a single vintage wine in 1985 and 1990.

Grand Siècle would never be advertised on TV nowadays, but in 1975 French viewers were treated to Patrick Macnee, playing the part of Steed from *The Avengers* series, which had been off the air for six years. His assistant Tara King (Linda Thorson) despatches a group of villains with her umbrella, as Steed calmly opens a bottle of Grand Siècle. The advert apparently helped fund *The New Avengers*, which came out a year later.

As for de Nonancourt, whose two daughters are both actively involved: "He was a gentle giant of a man," recalls Hesketh. "You saw his passion for champagne, and it must have been amazing to have worked alongside him in the days he was building the House to what it is now."

TASTING NOTES

LAURENT-PERRIER BRUT NV

There is a lightness of touch and crisp precision to LP's flagship wine whose sales are over five million bottles. Around half of the blend is chardonnay, which adds to the peach and pear-like flavours with a hint of red apples too. Down the middle is a line of tingling acidity.

LAURENT-PERRIER ROSÉ 2010

The colour may not matter to LP's David Hesketh, but it is an undeniably pretty shade of salmon pink, and it's hard to taste a fruit salad of red cherries, strawberries and the like. What is undeniable is the super-fine, creamy *mousse* and the mineral, wet-pebble finish.

ABOVE Bernard de Nonancourt's daughters – Alexandra Pereyre (left) and Stéphanie Meneux de Nonancourt – are key shareholders and actively involved in the business.

OPPOSITE Laurent-Perrier was one of the pioneers of bone dry champagne with its "Sans-Sucre" label in the UK in the late 19th century.

MOËT & CHANDON

ÉPERNAY

SOMEBODY SOMEWHERE IS CRACKING OPEN A BOTTLE OF MOËT & CHANDON EVERY SIX SECONDS IT IS POPULARLY ACCLAIMED. PRECISELY HOW MUCH IS SOLD IS KEPT SECRET, BUT SALES OF ITS MOËT IMPÉRIAL BRUT NV MUST BE WELL OVER 20 MILLION BOTTLES A YEAR. THAT'S AN AWFUL LOT OF BUBBLES.

Moët is nothing if not imperial. It is the flagship fizz of the mighty LVMH Moët Hennessy Louis Vuitton, which dominates the champagne trade. It also links directly to the Emperor himself since Napoleon was a lifelong customer, then friend of Jean-Rémy Moët, the grandson of Claude Moët who founded the House in 1743. Moët & Chandon were one of the first to embrace sparkling champagne in a region long wedded to still wines, and Claude Moët supplied the court of Versailles when the champagne-loving Madame de Pompadour was Louis XV's favourite.

Jean-Rémy Moët took over in 1792, when the French were revolting. The wine survived any guilt by association with the *Ancien Régime*, and Jean-Rémy was supplying Napoleon and Josephine by 1801.

Napoleon would stock up with champagne whenever passing through on his next military campaign. In 1814 Jean-Rémy was awarded the *Légion d'Honneur* for organising the defence and resistance of Épernay against the Cossacks, scouts of the Russian troops, thus allowing Napoleon to reach Épernay before the Allied armies. He also opened his cellars in order to preserve his neighbour's properties.

Jean-Rémy died in 1841, leaving the firm to his son, Victor Moët, and son-in-law, Comte Pierre-Gabriel Chandon, who had bought the ruined Abbey of Hautvillers and its vineyards some 20 years earlier. By the turn of the century, visitors would gasp at the industrial scale of Moët's champagne factory in Épernay with its 1,500 workers. George Kessler, the firm's US agent, boasted record imports of 102,000 cases in 1902 – more than a quarter of Moët's worldwide sales. Kessler was famed for his lavish parties in New York and London, and once flooded the Savoy's courtyard to create a Venetian lagoon stocked with live swans, ducks and sea trout. Enrico Caruso serenaded guests as they guzzled champagne aboard a giant gondola. The evening ended with a baby elephant bearing an enormous cake.

From this peak of conspicuous consumption, the brand

ABOVE Third-generation Jean-Rémy Moët took over in 1792, and built the foundations of the most powerful Champagne House of all, with a little help from his lifelong friend – Napoleon Bonaparte.

RIGHT Château de Saran, built in 1801 near the village of Chouilly by Jean-Rémy Moët, is where the House now entertains its top clients and guests.

BELOW The industrial might of the Moët & Chandon champagne factory in Épernay was something to behold in late-nineteenth-century France.

slipped into decline until Comte Robert-Jean de Vogüé entered the company in 1932 and soon took over. He proved a dynamic and inspirational leader for Moët & Chandon and champagne in general. Vogüé was bold enough to launch the luxurious *prestige cuvée* Dom Pérignon in 1936 despite the economic gloom, and represented the industry during the war, dealing with Hitler's *weinführer*, Otto Klaebisch. He also negotiated a substantial increase in grape prices to help the growers and champagne's long-term sustainability.

According to Moët & Chandon's International Marketing & Communications Director, Arnaud de Saignes, Vogüé was "among the first business leaders to realise the impact of public relations and star power". Maurice Chevalier, once the highest-paid actor in Hollywood, was courted to sprinkle some stardust on Vogüé's brands.

Before long it wasn't just Moët and Dom Pérignon, as the company acquired first Mercier in 1970, Ruinart in 1973, and also Parfums Christian Dior in 1971. Today LVMH controls around one-fifth of all champagne and some two-thirds of the US market.

"We like to say 'bigger is better'," says Arnaud de Saignes, referring to the firm's 1,180 hectares of vineyards that supply over one-third of Moët's needs. Benoît Gouez, the brand's respected *chef de cave*, insists quality and quantity are not mutually exclusive in champagne. LVMH inspires respect among rivals, given the group's continued success and growth.

There are rumours that the group intends to grow its production from 60 to 100 million bottles. It is an unresolved question where they will they find all the grapes, and whether any other Champagne Houses will lose out as a result.

ABOVE Tennis legend Roger Federer bringing his charm, sophistication and savoir-faire to his role as the global brand ambassador of Moët & Chandon.

BELOW Bottles lie *sur lattes* in Moët's cellars, slowly transforming into champagne. The firm's cellars are the largest in the region, stretching for 17 miles beneath the streets of Épernay.

CHAMPAGNE MOUSSEUX. SILLERY MOUSSEUX SUPÉRIEUR. CRÉMANT D'AY, ROSÉ. GRAND CRÉMANT IMPÉRIAL. WHITE STAR (SEC). BRUT IMPÉRIAL (EXTRA SEC).

TOP Within Moët's early range, White Star was sold as a demi-sec with 20g/l of sugar in the American market until it was withdrawn in 2012.

ABOVE A First World War cartoon that translates roughly as: "Well old man, you were hoping to take Champagne were you? In that case, have a cork instead!"

TASTING NOTES

MOËT & CHANDON
IMPERIAL BRUT NV

The flagship of Moët & Chandon since 1869, Brut Imperial is renowned the world over for its complexity and consistency. Golden straw yellow in colour with green highlights, it is characterised by a bright fruitiness, a richly flavourful palate and an elegant maturity, that continually seduce and delight.

MOËT & CHANDON
GRAND VINTAGE ROSÉ 2008

Moët has been producing vintage rosé for over 40 years, and this latest expression is a wine of great succulence and fullness, with floral notes of rose and hawthorn; botanical nuances of boxwood and lime zest; and fruity, fresh notes of raspberry, cherry and blood orange.

LEFT AND ABOVE There's plenty of Art Deco nostalgia in this UK ad campaign from the 1970s.

G.H. MUMM
REIMS

WITH ITS CUDDLY BRAND NAME, AND EASILY RECOGNISABLE LABEL, MUMM CORDON ROUGE HAS BEEN A TOP-SELLING CHAMPAGNE SINCE THE 1900s, WHEN IT WAS EVERYWHERE FROM HOTEL BARS IN NEW ZEALAND TO THE BROTHELS OF NEW ORLEANS. AFTER A RECENT BAD PATCH, IT APPEARS TO BE BACK ON FORM UNDER PERNOD RICARD.

"Wine flowed much more than water did during those periods," recalled the jazz legend Jelly Roll Morton in the 1930s about New Orleans at the turn of the century. "The kind of wine I'm speaking about, I don't mean sauternes or nothing like that, I mean champagne … among the main ones were Clicquot, which is a French wine, and Mumm's Extra Dry … that was an English wine."

While Morton may have become muddled about that last point, he was right about the names. Mumm was a massive brand thanks to its flagship Cordon Rouge, launched by Georges Hermann von Mumm in 1876. With its famous red sash label, as though bestowed with the *Légion d'Honneur* by the President himself, it was distinctive and easy to remember. It flowed through every whorehouse and jazz joint on New Orleans's Basin Street, and far beyond. By 1902 it was selling more than one million cases in the States out of more than three million worldwide, almost one-tenth of champagne's total sales.

The firm was established in Reims in 1827 by Georges Hermann's father and two uncles, who had crossed over from the Rhineland where the Mumms were well-established wine merchants and vineyard owners. The family began buying plots in Champagne, starting with Verzenay in 1840, where they were one of the first to instal a press house beside the vineyards to crush the grapes before they lost freshness.

For what they bought in from the growers, they preferred to buy grapes rather than fermented wine like most of their rivals.

By 1913, G. H. Mumm owned around 50 hectares, mainly in the Côte des Blancs. Unfortunately the owners had failed to take out French citizenship like the other Houses of German origin, and the whole company was confiscated by the state on the outbreak of war. In 1920 it was sold at auction to a consortium that included the Dubonnets, whose son-in-law, René Lalou, was appointed a director. As a young Parisian lawyer he knew nothing of the champagne trade, but he learnt fast, and became the real driving force behind the brand for almost 50 years. Thanks to the salesmanship of Georges Hermann in the late nineteenth century, Cordon Rouge was one of the first global champagnes, drunk from Sydney to San Francisco.

The original Mumms didn't quite give up on their brand, and briefly requisitioned it during the Second World War. René Lalou was soon back in charge, however, and being an avid art collector, commissioned the Japanese artist Léonard Foujita to design the rose on the top of Mumm's new rosé champagne, launched in 1957. By then Seagram, the giant US spirits producer, had begun to buy into the brand, followed by Perrier-Jouët and Heidsieck Monopole. Before long they controlled Mumm outright, and this gave it a hefty

ABOVE Second-generation Georges Hermann Mumm was responsible for launching Cordon Rouge, with its distinctive red sash label, in 1876. By the end of the century global sales were topping three million bottles.

BELOW LEFT The headquarters of G.H. Mumm & Cie in Reims – the House founded by a family of German winemakers from the Rhineland in 1827.

BELOW The Moulin de Verzenay, a famous landmark by the grand cru village of Verzenay, in the Montagne de Reims, overlooks some of Mumm's 218 hectares of vineyards.

boost in distribution. In the UK it was almost always on promotion through the Oddbins chain that Seagram owned.

Cordon Rouge was famed for its fresh, floral, easy-going style with a lightness that belied its dominant grape – pinot noir. The variety accounts for almost 80% of the 218 hectares owned by Mumm, 160 of them in eight Grand Cru villages including Aÿ, Bouzy, Verzenay and Cramant. The special Cuvée René Lalou, a 50:50 blend of pinot noir and chardonnay from these villages, was first released in the 1960s, only to be dropped before Seagram sold the business. Since 2006 Mumm has been back in French hands, alongside Perrier-Jouët, under Pernod Ricard.

In the meantime, the old Lalou-inspired *cuvée* has been reinstated, and with its spicy, fulsome, almost buttery style, it's quite different to Mumm's main expression. Cordon Rouge went through a lean patch in the late twentieth century and some pesky British journalists declared its Californian offshoot Mumm Cuvée Napa, at half the price, was better in blind tastings. They were told, with wonderful Gallic distain, not to compare blondes with brunettes. Today's Mumm Cordon Rouge is infinitely better thanks to cellar master Didier Mariotti and his team. And, after 15 years of being sprayed from the podiums of Formula One, it now sponsors Formula E – the world's first all-electric racing series.

LA PLUS HAUTE QUALITÉ
caractérise
LES CHAMPAGNES G.H. MUMM & Cⁱᵉ
SOCIÉTÉ VINICOLE DE CHAMPAGNE PROPRIÉTAIRE
REIMS

TOP LEFT At the dawn of the 20th century Mumm could barely keep up with a global demand of 3 million cases.

ABOVE A poster from the 1930s for Mumm's flagship brand. Note the none-too-subtle nod to a certain popular brand of soft drink.

TASTING NOTES

MUMM CORDON ROUGE BRUT NV

Hugely popular in France, Cordon Rouge accounts for around 90% of Mumm's production. With a well-judged *dosage* of 9g/l, compared to around 12g in the past, it has a nervy freshness to balance the soft texture of its predominantly black fruit with the blend 45% pinot noir and 25% pinot meunier.

MUMM BRUT MILLÉSIMÉ 2006

While Cordon Rouge is about softness and approachability, Mumm 2006 is built to last despite the ripeness of fruit thanks to early summer heat and a perfect September. The blend of two-thirds pinot noir to one-third chardonnay is aged for five years on the lees, and then given a low *dosage* of just 6g/l.

LEFT A few of the five million bottles of Mumm produced each year – this batch seemingly from the grand cru village of Bouzy, where the House owns vineyards.

PERRIER-JOUËT
ÉPERNAY

THE SWIRLING IMAGERY AROUND PERRIER-JOUËT AND THE BEAUTIFUL ENAMELLED BELLE ÉPOQUE BOTTLES DATES FROM THE HEIGHT OF THE ART NOUVEAU MOVEMENT IN PARIS. THE DESIGN ENCAPSULATES THE FLOWERY ELEGANCE OF THE WINE, YET IT TOOK UNTIL THE LATE 1960s FOR IT TO FINALLY APPEAR IN PUBLIC.

For Pierre Bezukhov, in Tolstoy's *War and Peace*, the Great Comet of 1811 was a bad omen, perhaps signalling the end of the world. But for newly weds Pierre-Nicolas Perrier and Rose-Adélaïde Jouët, it was a symbol of hope for the champagne business they had just founded. This feeling was reinforced by that year's exceptional vintage.

Demand for it allowed the couple to buy premises at the prosaic-sounding 24 Rue du Commerce in Épernay. By the end of the century it was the Avenue de Champagne, the smartest street in town, while Perrier-Jouët had become immensely popular. The man who really laid the foundations was their son, Charles Perrier, who took over in 1848. He was also mayor of Épernay and a member of parliament.

By the 1850s he was wealthy enough to commission the imposing Château Perrier across the street from his HQ where he could entertain Napoleon III and his wife, the Empress Eugénie. The first bottles of Perrier-Jouët arrived in England as early as 1815, just months after the Battle of Waterloo, while shipments to America followed in 1837.

A decade later, the firm's UK agent tried to pioneer bone-dry champagne with a *Zéro Dosage* bottling, but without success. The English fashion for Brut only really started in the 1870s, by which point Perrier-Jouët was in great demand across the Channel, Britain soon accounting for 90% of sales. Among its fans were Queen Victoria, Edward the Prince of Wales, Oscar Wilde and 'the most famous actress the world has ever known'. This was the French star of stage and silent screen Sarah Bernhardt, who liked to bathe in Perrier-Jouët, or so it was claimed.

Charles Perrier died in 1878, leaving a thriving business to his nephew, Henri Gallice. The Franco-Prussian War had ended and Europe entered a sustained period of peace and prosperity that was looked back on with deep nostalgia after the horrors of the First World War. Culture and the arts flourished, especially in Paris, where the era became known as the Belle Époque. Its spirit was captured in a beautifully decorated bottle of the same name.

It was in 1902 that Émile Gallé, a master glassmaker and leading light in the Art Nouveau movement, was approached by Henri

ABOVE Rose Adélaïde-Jouët (top) and her husband Pierre-Nicolas Perrier (below), co-founded the House in 1811, the year of the Great Comet, which proved to be an auspicious omen. But, in reality, it was their son Charles Perrier who built the brand and the family's reputation.

LEFT Like Moët & Chandon and Pol Roger, Perrier-Jouët is another grand resident of Épernay's smartest street – the Avenue de Champagne.

Gallice to design a bottle for his vintage champagne. The artist was also a renowned botanist and chose a spray of white Japanese anemones from his garden, apparently to reflect the colour and floral nature of chardonnay. Unfortunately there was no way to replicate Gallé's art on any scale and the idea was abandoned. It was not until the *chef de cave*, André Bavaret, discovered the original bottles in a cupboard in the 1960s that it was decided to copy the designs and launch the Belle Époque vintage *cuvée* in 1969 to celebrate Duke Ellington's 70th birthday in Paris. Some 500 privileged customers were given a numbered magnum each, and the rest were sold through Maxim's and Fauchon, the city's swankiest food store. In time Belle Époque was followed by a rosé and a Blanc de Blancs.

By now the House was run by a family cousin Michel Budin, though ownership had passed to Seagram, who also owned Champagne Mumm. This boosted PJ's distribution, especially in the US where "hardly an episode of *Dallas* goes by without JR Ewing knocking back a bottle," wrote Don Hewitson in *The Glory of Champagne*.

Seagram's drinks empire was broken up and Perrier-Jouët found itself passed around until finally settling with Pernod-Ricard in 2006. It is back in French hands, albeit those of a drinks giant best known for spirits like Chivas Regal, Jameson's and Absolut. In 2008 an über-premium Blanc de Blancs from a grand cru single vineyard in Cramant was added, priced at a breathtaking £35,000 a case. But you did get to chose the *dosage* to make it bespoke.

Today Perrier-Jouët owns 65 hectares of vineyards, more than half in the Côte des Blancs – enough to supply a quarter of its needs. The current *chef de cave*, Hervé Deschamps, seeks the crisp elegance of chardonnay married to the flesh and perfume of pinot noir to create the house style.

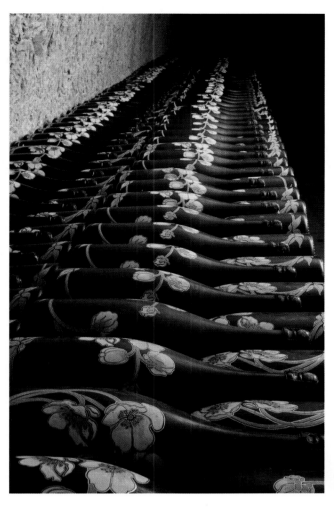

TASTING NOTES

PERRIER-JOUËT GRAND BRUT NV

There's a buttery softness to the black fruit (40% pinot noir and 40% pinot meunier) freshened up with lemon zest and a fruity, peach-like core. With 30 months on the lees and a 9g/l dosage, it's not be hugely complex but has a hazy, soft-focused charm.

PERRIER-JOUËT BELLE EPOQUE 2007

Beautiful Belle Epoque, is a hefty step up in price and you're obviously paying something for those Art Nouveau anemones, but it is a lovely champagne with its richness and purity of fruit. It somehow manages to be bright and precise and gentle all at the same time.

ABOVE LEFT Belle Époque bottles, in all their glory, resting in the cellars of Perrier-Jouët. The original Art Nouveau design from 1902 could not be reproduced on any scale, and was not publicly released until 1969.

LEFT Traditional *pupitres* are on display in virtually every Champagne House, though the vast majority of bottles are now riddled by machine in giant *gyropalletes* that few visitors get to see.

PHILIPPONNAT

MAREUIL-SUR-AŸ

THE PHILIPPONNATS HAVE BEEN GROWERS AND *NÉGOCIANTS* IN CHAMPAGNE FOR ALMOST FIVE CENTURIES, THOUGH IT IS ONLY IN THE PAST 50 YEARS THAT THE BRAND HAS SOARED, THANKS TO ITS FAMOUS SINGLE VINEYARD CHAMPAGNE. IT MAY BE CORPORATELY OWNED, BUT IT FEELS EVERY INCH A FAMILY-RUN HOUSE.

Charles Philipponnat certainly has pedigree when it comes to champagne. As CEO of the eponymous house, he can trace his family's roots back to 1522, when an ancestor gave up his military career as a Swiss mercenary captain and settled in Aÿ with his own vineyards. By the end of the following century his descendants were supplying red wine to the court of the Sun King, Louis XIV. Quite when they began making sparkling wine is unclear.

The Philipponnats never moved, except to the neighbouring village of Mareuil-sur-Aÿ in 1910. Twenty-five years later, Charles' great uncle bought 5.5 hectares of semi-abandoned vineyards that had been part of the former cellars of the Château de Mareuil, and whose owners had gone bankrupt. If this steep, south-facing plot, surrounded by walls as though it were in Burgundy, was in any way famous, it was because of an old postcard photograph. It showed the vineyards reflected in the Marne canal to resemble a champagne bottle lying on its side.

This was Les Clos des Goisses, which has become home to arguably the most highly regarded single vineyard champagne of them all. "Only about a third was in production, as no-one wanted to break their backs cultivating it," says Charles explaining how his great uncle was able to buy it for a relatively modest sum. A Clos des Goisses champagne was soon released, but it was only when the worn-out vines were replanted with Pinot Noir in 1964 that the true potential began to emerge.

Positioned to soak up as much sunshine as possible with the angle of the slope as much as 45° in parts, temperatures in this sheltered vineyard are 1.5°C higher than the regional average. This appears to suit the Burgundian black grape perfectly with Clos de Goisses two-thirds Pinot Noir and one-third Chardonnay. Its ripeness is just what Charles Philipponnat desires. "I believe quality in Champagne is about ripe grapes," he says. "It's about good fruit that you can eat."

He accepts global warming as a reality, but sees it as a positive for Champagne. "I think with Clos des Goisses we have proof that we can grow riper grapes and still make very good wine," he says. "I believe temperature is only one element of *terroir,* and not the main one, which is soil. If champagne has any problem today, it's with unripeness." The grapes are picked at the peak of physiological ripeness which means the juice is relatively low in acidity. Yet, somehow, the chalky soil and the lack of malolactic fermentation in the cellar helps what little acidity there is to shine through, especially given the wine's low *dosage.* Clos des Goisses has been Extra-Brut for more than 20 years.

But for the Chardonnay found here, Philipponnat's other vineyards are all planted with Pinot Noir which thrives on the south-facing slopes around Aÿ in the heart of Champagne where the Vallée de la Marne, the Montange de Reims and the Côtes des Blancs converge.

RIGHT Charles Philipponnat in his cellar.

BELOW The famous champagne bottle postcard of "Les Goisses".

Mareuil-sur-Ay — LES GOISSES

Curieux effet d'un des meilleurs crus de la Champagne, qui donne par sa forme et son reflet sur les eaux du Canal de la Marne au Rhin, l'illusion de la Bouteille de Champagne
Garanti sans aucun truquage

Champagne PHILIPPONNAT
Le Clos des Goisses - Circa 1908

TASTING NOTES

PHILIPPONNAT ROYALE RÉSERVE NV BRUT

This is a relatively rich style of NV, led by ripe pinot noir that accounts for two-thirds of the blend, the rest being mostly chardonnay. Yet there's a freshness, too, coupled with some subtle spice and nutty flavours making for a fine aperitif champagne.

PHILIPPONNAT CLOS DES GOISSES 2009

An intense, aromatic champagne with a nose of ripe pears, stone fruit and beeswax. A persistent bead of tiny bubbles coats the tongue in a creamy, elegant mousse, while its sumptuous and complex palette slowly gives way to a bone-dry finish.

LEFT The house ages its wines in the magnificent 18th century cellars of the Château de Mareuil.

BELOW By the early 18th century the Philipponnat family was supplying red wine to the court of Louis XIV.

In total the house owns 17 hectares and cultivates another five, accounting for one-third of its needs for a production of around 700,000 bottles. "We buy our grapes mostly from around here," says Charles, who describes the house style as follows: "It's about intensity of flavour and fruit from mainly ripe pinot noir, with a freshness and minerality that comes naturally from the soil." The result is lighter than the big, bold pinot noir styles of champagnes such as Bollinger.

"I don't feel proud of Champagne Philipponnat, I feel responsible," says Charles about the family legacy, even if the firm is now part of the same group that owns Lanson. It was acquired in 1997, three years before he joined, having been a vice president at Moët & Chandon. This begs the question – just how independent is Philipponnat? "101%!" replies Charles in a flash. "I have my own grapes, my own vineyards, my own winery, my own financing and my own distribution network."

This hands-off approach by the parent group – Lanson BCC – appears to work well, and may endure if the next generation of Philipponnats are up for the challenge.

PIPER-HEIDSIECK

REIMS

WITH ITS VOLUPTUOUS RED AND GOLD LABEL, PIPER-HEIDSIECK HAS LONG SOUGHT TO STAND OUT FROM THE CROWD, AND NOT LEAST THE OTHER HEIDSIECK CHAMPAGNES DOING THE ROUNDS. IT IS A SOMEWHAT CONVOLUTED STORY, BUT ONE FULL OF COLOUR AND ENRICHED BY SOME GOOD, OLD-FASHIONED HOLLYWOOD GLAMOUR.

The first time Marilyn Monroe was asked what she wore in bed, her response was considered too salacious to print. The shocking truth emerged in 1952, when readers of *Life* magazine discovered that she slept in nothing but a drop of Chanel No. 5. "And I wake up to a glass of Piper-Heidsieck," she would sometimes add to what became a stock interview question. Yet the image of a naked, perfumed Marilyn between the sheets was so irresistible, certainly to Chanel's marketing team, that the champagne reference was often glossed over.

Still there is no doubt Marilyn Monroe loved her champagne, and especially Piper-Heidsieck, then one of the biggest-selling brands in the United States. She was said to keep a month's supply of it in her kitchen to make sure she never ran out. The champagne was well in with the big Hollywood studios, having first appeared in the movies in Laurel and Hardy's *Sons of the Desert* in 1933. Today Piper-Heidsieck supplies the Oscars ceremony and has sponsored the Cannes Film Festival every year since the early 1990s.

What was originally known as Champagne Heidsieck was established in 1785, when there were probably fewer than 10 Champagne Houses in existence. Its founder Florenz-Ludwig (later to become Florens-Louis) Heidsieck dealt in fine fabrics, which he supplied to the courtiers of Versailles among others. He used to travel from his home in Westphalia in Germany to Reims, one of the key textile towns in northern France. On one of these visits he fell in love with a local girl and decided to settle in Reims. After dabbling in champagne production for a few years, he set up his own House.

When his only child died young, Florens-Louis invited his nephews to join him in business. One of them, Charles-Henri Heidsieck, had famously ridden on a white stallion to Moscow ahead of Napoleon's advancing army, with a stash of champagne to sell to the winning side. Talk about opportunism! When old man Heidsieck died in 1828, the family firm began to fragment. In 1834 two nephews left to establish what became Heidsieck Monopole, leaving Christian Heidsieck to carry on with his partner, André-Guillaume Piper. Christian died a year later, and his widow then married Piper after a suitable period of mourning. Because the US market had taken to calling the brand Piper's Heidsieck, the House was officially rechristened Piper-Heidsieck in 1845.

But as if this wasn't enough to confuse people, Charles-Henri's son, Charles-Camille, whose mother was from the House of Henriot, decided that he too would launch a champagne in 1851. Given that Charles Heidsieck and Piper-Heidsieck are now owned by the same firm, it makes sense to combine the two stories. Charles

ABOVE Charles-Camille Heidsieck, otherwise known as Champagne Charlie, was the man who helped popularise champagne in the United States after his made his first trip there in 1852.

ABOVE Glitzy and glamorous – Piper-Heidsieck's distinctive red and gold label is made for Tinseltown. It supplies the Oscars ceremony and has been a long-term sponsor of the Cannes Film Festival.

RIGHT Marilyn Monroe was a huge fan of the brand. It was rumoured that she kept a month's supply of Piper-Heidsieck in her kitchen, to avoid running out.

LEFT Pages from Charles Heidsieck's accounts ledger for sales of its champagne to the United States in 1935–36. It was just after the end of Prohibition, which lasted between 1920 and 1933. It took a few years for sales to return to its pre World War 1 levels.

BELOW LEFT A magazine advert from the 1950s with a rather orange-looking glass of fizz. In time Piper realised it needed bolder packaging to stand out from those other Heidsieck champagnes.

BELOW Bottles resting *sur latte*.

TASTING NOTES

PIPER-HEIDSIECK BRUT NV

The blend of Piper's flagship champagne is almost a Blanc de Noirs, with just 15% chardonnay, but the style is lighter and fresher than that suggests. It has appealingly bright, lively fruit with a distinct flavour of lemon zest and the aromas of a French *pâtisserie*.

PIPER-HEIDSIECK RARE MILLÉSIME 2002

Piper's Régis Camus and winemaker Séverine Frerson-Gomez excelled with this magnificent vintage. The blend, 70% chardonnay / 30% pinot noir from the Montagne de Reims, is finely balanced and manages a brittle precision like meringue and yet a generous, dried-fruit core. It has the silkiest *mousse* of bubbles and a lingering mineral finish.

Heidsieck certainly stole the limelight with his exploits in America, where he first went in 1852. He was the original 'Champagne Charlie' who helped build US sales of fizz to over 300,000 bottles by the outbreak of the American Civil War, at which point his US agent stitched him up.

Charlie headed down to New Orleans to recover his debts, but got embroiled in the war and was nearly hanged as a Confederate spy. He finally returned home, a broken man until he suddenly received the property deeds to a third of Denver, from the brother of the US agent in an act of atonement. As Denver blossomed into a boomtown, Charlie made a fortune and his champagne business re-sparkled into life. If Champagne Charlie sounds like a movie, it is, though the 1989 rom-com starring Hugh Grant didn't do the story justice.

Yet Piper-Heidsieck became far bigger in America thanks to J. C. Kunkelmann, a long-term partner who inherited the House in 1870. Over time it passed to his granddaughter Yolande, who married the Marquis Jean de Suarez d'Aulan in 1926. As a pioneer aviator, bobsleigh champion and Resistance hero during the war, he sounds like another film script. The Marquis escaped the Gestapo by the skin of his teeth, only to be shot down in his plane above Alsace in 1945. Piper-Heidsieck was run by his son for 33 years, and since 2011 has belonged to the Descours family.

POL ROGER
ÉPERNAY

"REMEMBER, GENTLEMEN, IT'S NOT JUST FRANCE WE ARE FIGHTING FOR, IT'S CHAMPAGNE!"
DECLARED WINSTON CHURCHILL IN A FAMOUS RALLYING CALL TO THE TROOPS DURING THE
SECOND WORLD WAR. WHICH WAS MORE IMPORTANT – THE COUNTRY OR THE DRINK – IS A
MOOT POINT.

One imagines Churchill believed France was worth saving without
its fizz, but perhaps not with quite the same enthusiasm. He
certainly loved champagne, especially Pol Roger. If he was on two
bottles a day since his first order for Pol Roger in 1908, as has
been claimed, he would have drunk 42,000 bottles in his lifetime,
or enough to float a battleship. Add in the morning drip feed of
dilute Johnnie Walker, dubbed 'Papa's cocktail', the early-evening
Scotches, the liquid dinner and the post-prandial brandies with a
highball to finish, and it make you wonder. It seems a miracle that
Churchill made it to middle age, let alone get Britain through its
'darkest hour'. Yet, like that other pub quiz favourite about the
250,000 cigars he allegedly smoked, the drink was probably at
least partly a prop to demonstrate his larger-than-life capacity for
booze and his cast-iron constitution.

Paul Roger, universally known as Pol, set up his wine business
in the family village of Aÿ in 1849. Within three years he had
moved to Épernay as Champagne Roger, which he ran until his
two sons took over in 1899. Georges and Maurice, who changed
the family name to Pol-Roger, inherited a thriving business with a
royal warrant from Queen Victoria granted in 1877. It was served
in the grand hotels along the Champs-Élysées and in London's
West End, and in the House of Commons, where Winston
Churchill possibly discovered it.

As mayor of Épernay, Maurice Pol-Roger had to cope with the
Germans when they marched into town on 4 September 1914.
He was held hostage and threatened with execution four times
before the Germans left a week later, having been defeated in the
Battle of the Marne. Pol-Roger and his friends at Perrier-Jouët
immediately set about organising the harvest as artillery shells
whizzed and roared in the background. And so it was throughout
the war, with grapes picked every vintage. While Épernay escaped
the devastation suffered by Reims, a hundred bombs fell one
summer's day in 1917, and the entire population took refuge in
the cellars of Pol Roger and Perrier-Jouët.

The Churchill connection was cemented in the next war at
a party in Paris after the city's liberation in August 1944. The
wartime leader was completely captivated by Odette Pol-Roger.
She was a renowned society beauty and Maurice's daughter-in-law.
Were they more than just good friends? "Well, I'm sure he fancied
her," says James Simpson, head of Pol Roger (UK). "But no, it
was 'a harmless, late autumn friendship' as someone called it."
Churchill promised to stamp the grapes with his own bare feet if
he were ever invited to what he called "the world's most drinkable
address". Sadly he never made it to Épernay, but Odette made
sure he was supplied with a case every birthday of his favourite
vintage – 1928 – until it ran out. In return he named his favourite

TOP As a medium-sized Champagne House, with an annual
production of 1.6 million bottles, Pol Roger's 91 hectares of vineyards
are enough to satisfy half of its needs.

ABOVE According to James Simpson, head of Pol Roger UK, Winston
Churchill was "a proper Edwardian gent who didn't like red or white
wine. He drank champagne by the pint in a silver tankard, two at
lunch and one for dinner."

racehorse Pol Roger in her honour.

The Champagne House responded in kind by releasing its Sir Winston Churchill vintage *cuvée* for the first time in 1975, 10 years after his death. A black border appeared on the label and remained there for years. The House came out of mourning only in 2003, when it won back the royal warrant that had lapsed in the 1930s. "Yet even now, we get some old codger complaining about us removing the armband," says Simpson.

The House is still in family hands, thanks in no small part to owning 91 hectares of vineyards, or half its needs for its 1.6 million bottle production. Simpson concedes there may be a slight over-reliance on one famous customer, but says:

> *"If all people ever remember about Pol Roger is that it's family-owned and Churchill drank it, that's a whole lot more than most other champagnes."*

Churchill certainly delighted in displaying his vices, unlike his biographer and one of his most ardent fans – Boris Johnson. While some say the Tory MP has Churchillian delusions of grandeur, you wouldn't catch him necking a bottle of Pol Roger in public.

ABOVE RIGHT Churchill named one of the racehorses he bred Pol Roger after Odette, the daughter-in-law of Maurice Pol Roger, whom he befriended after Paris was liberated in 1944.

BELOW The House's sumptuous head office in Épernay, at 44 Avenue Champagne, which, according to Churchill, was "the most drinkable address in the world".

BELOW RIGHT Churchill's telegram to Odette saying Pol Roger was running in a 1952 race.

TASTING NOTES

POL ROGER BRUT RÉSERVE NV

Pol Roger bills this wine as "'the perfect apéritif champagne", and it certainly has the fresh, youthful vigour to sharpen the taste buds. The elegance is supplied by the third that is Côte des Blancs chardonnay, while an equal measure of Montage de Reims pinot noir adds to the crunchy red apple fruit.

POL ROGER BRUT VINTAGE 2006

Selecting the best fruit at its disposal, all grands crus, this marriage is led by pinot noir from the Montagne and 40% chardonnay from the Côte, which gives the wine its lemony core and chalky, mineral edge. Add in flavours of red apple, almond croissants, a dusting of vanilla … and it's fairly irresistible.

Telegram to
Madame Pol Roger
7, Avenue Emile Accolas,
Paris, VII, France.

   Pol Roger runs today over
hurdles for the first time and
is well fancied.   Am putting
a fiver on each way for you.
                 WINSTON.

Despatched 20/iv/52

POMMERY
REIMS

LOUISE POMMERY WAS A FORCE OF NATURE NOT UNLIKE THE MIGHTY VEUVE CLICQUOT. YOU MIGHT NOT GUESS FROM HER WIDOW'S WEEDS AND STERN EXPRESSION IN HER PORTRAITS, BUT SHE PROVED TO BE ONE OF THE MOST FLAMBOYANT BRAND-BUILDERS IN THE HISTORY OF CHAMPAGNE.

Veuve Clicquot was a big brand by the mid-nineteenth century with sales of more than 400,000 bottles a year, and its namesake, the widow Barbe Nicole, still very much involved in her seventies. Soon a new champagne widow was on the scene, every bit as determined as Veuve Clicquot herself.

The story starts with a small Champagne House called Dubois-Gosset, which Narcisse Greno took over in 1836. While Greno took care of sales and marketing, the financial backing came from Louis Alexandre Pommery, scion of a wealthy textile family in Reims. Pommery came to own the majority of the House and when he died in 1858, his widow Louise assumed control.

Veuve Pommery was approaching 40, while the firm of Pommery & Greno was more into wool than wine, the latter more still than sparkling. Louise soon changed that as she and her faithful assistant, Henri Vasnier, propelled Champagne Pommery into the big time. It became particularly popular in the UK, where it helped pioneer the taste for *brut* champagne.

Her physical legacy is the company's colossal, castle-like HQ on the eastern side of Reims. It sits above 18 kilometres of cellars and tunnels carved out of the *crayères*, or chalk and limestone quarries dug by the Romans, which she bought from the Ruinarts. Claude Ruinart had simply stored his wine there, but Madame Pommery decided to turn them into a 'Theatre of Champagne' that became one of the top tourist attractions in France. The scale and industrial self-confidence of the enterprise recalls Victorian shipyards on the Clyde, though it has to be said champagne has endured rather better.

Visitors gasped at the collection of turrets and spires – an architectural pick 'n' mix of Scots Baronial and Disneyland – before descending a grand staircase into the cellar. There are bas-reliefs carved into the walls and vast wooden blending vats. Bottles stretch off into the gloom along boulevards named after some of the key cities Pommery supplied: Dublin, Buenos Aires and Havana.

Meanwhile, above ground, Madame Pommery had begun to accumulate vineyards and to wean the British on to *brut*-style champagne. "Damas, we need a wine that is as dry as possible, but without rigidity," she wrote to her *chef de cave*, Olivier Damas. "It should be soft and velvety on the palate … Above all, make sure it has finesse." The wine, created by his successor, Victor Lambert, was

ABOVE The redoubtable Madame Louise Pommery, who inherited the House in 1858, and went on to become one of the great champagne widows in the mould of Veuve Clicquot.

ABOVE The sprawling headquarters of Champagne Pommery on the eastern outskirts of Reims, resembles Walt Disney's Magic Kingdom.

RIGHT Rare bottles of vintage Pommery in the House's cellar. Today Pommery produces somewhere in the region of five million bottles of champagne per annum.

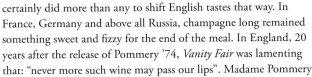

Champagne POMMERY & GRENO - Reims

F. Rothier, phot. - Reims
35 Les Caves Pommery à Reims — Le Grand escalier

TASTING NOTES

POMMERY BRUT ROYAL NV

Pommery recently went through something of a lean patch, but it has much improved under new owners Vranken. The boldly packaged Brut Royal is a classic apéritif style that is delicate, ethereal, and gently floral on the nose with a taut, lively core of cranberry and redcurrant fruit.

POMMERY BRUT ROSÉ NV

The same cranberry flavours are there in the rosé that is made from bleeding the colour from the black grapes in a brief moment of skin contact. The winemaker has carefully avoided any tannin seeping in, and there's an earthy, mineral note behind the refreshing red fruit core.

the 1874 Pommery *Nature* that was sold in England two years later.

Whether Pommery "invented" *brut* or not, this particular bottle certainly did more than any to shift English tastes that way. In France, Germany and above all Russia, champagne long remained something sweet and fizzy for the end of the meal. In England, 20 years after the release of Pommery '74, *Vanity Fair* was lamenting that: "never more such wine may pass our lips". Madame Pommery died in 1890, having married her daughter Louise to Prince Guy de Polignac, who was as blue-blooded as they come and cousin to Monaco's ruling family, the Grimaldis.

With global sales of more than two million bottles and pole position in the UK, Pommery was in fine shape for the next generation that included Louis Pommery, his sister Louise and her well-connected husband. Between them they expanded the vineyards to 300 hectares, second only to the holding of Moët & Chandon.

By 1907 the next generation – Melchior de Polignac – was in charge and it remained in his descendants' hands until 1979, when the fertiliser tycoon Xavier Gardinier bought Pommery and Lanson. All members of the family were culled from the business apart from Alain de Polignac, who remained as winemaker, and who later created the luxury Cuvée Louise in honour of the famous widow.

Owning Lanson and Pommery proved too much, and the Gardiniers sold out to the French multinational BSN in 1984, who in turn sold both brands to LVMH six years later. Lanson was soon sold again, while Pommery was taken over by Paul-François Vranken in 2002, but it had lost control of its vineyards. Today, with Heidsieck-Monopole and Vranken Champagne as stablemates, Pommery is in strong hands.

T.TRIPETTE Phot ·REIMS

BRETA

TOP LEFT Part of the chalk and limestone quarries dug by the Romans, which were used as cellars by the Ruinart family and then sold to Champagne Pommery.

TOP MIDDLE Pommery's vast army of 'cellar rats' on the grand staircase descending into the bowels of the earth beneath Reims. Dubbed the Theatre of Champagne, it became one of France's top tourist attractions.

ABOVE LEFT In July 1868, work began on transforming a number of ancient chalk quarries into the cellars of Maison Pommery. It was the greatest construction project of the 19th century in Reims.

LEFT A modern art installation within the 18 kilometres of tunnels owned by Pommery, and connected by boulevards named after key cities the House supplied.

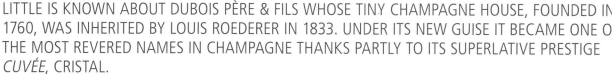

LOUIS ROEDERER

REIMS

LITTLE IS KNOWN ABOUT DUBOIS PÈRE & FILS WHOSE TINY CHAMPAGNE HOUSE, FOUNDED IN 1760, WAS INHERITED BY LOUIS ROEDERER IN 1833. UNDER ITS NEW GUISE IT BECAME ONE OF THE MOST REVERED NAMES IN CHAMPAGNE THANKS PARTLY TO ITS SUPERLATIVE PRESTIGE *CUVÉE*, CRISTAL.

Unlike most of his fellow merchants, Roederer believed in acquiring vineyards at a time when grape prices were so low it seemed to make little economic sense to do so. "I think he had this vision of making the best champagne possible, and the way to do that was to own your own vineyards in the best *grand cru* sites," believes Frédéric Rouzard, the current boss and now the seventh generation in charge. Of his ancestor's first purchase – 15 hectares in Verzenay – he says: "Today they're recognised as one of the best sites for pinot noir in Champagne."

Rouzard has added another 25 hectares to bring Roederer's current total to around 240 hectares. They stretch from the south-facing slopes of the Marne valley in Mareuil, Aÿ and other villages, to top chardonnay sites in the Côte des Blancs, and the pinot noir heartlands of the Montagne de Reims. With a production of around 3 million bottles a year, the firm's own grapes supply 70% of its requirements, and all its needs in the case of its vintage wines. More than two-thirds of the vineyards are grand cru.

When his great-grandmother, the formidable Camille Olry-Roederer, was on the prowl for new vineyards in the 1930s there were growers desperate to sell. Today it has become a great deal harder, as Rouzard concedes. With grapes now selling for up to €6 a kilo, the asking price for even a couple of rows of grand cru vines has reached eye-popping levels. Rivals with fewer vineyards might suggest the secret to great champagne lies more in the cellar where the *cuvées* are constructed, than in the land. Yet behind the scenes one suspects they covet Roederer's magnificent estate – and quite right too.

By the second half of the nineteenth century, champagne's biggest foreign customers after the British were the Russians. It was a market first developed by Veuve Clicquot and her salesman Louis Bohn, but despite their best efforts other champagnes seeped in, including Louis Roederer. In the 1870s the House was asked to create an exclusive *cuvée* for the Russian Emperor, Alexander II. The best and oldest vineyards were selected, but all their goodness was buried beneath a ton of sugar by the time Cristal was presented to

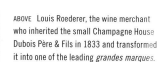

ABOVE Louis Roederer, the wine merchant who inherited the small Champagne House Dubois Père & Fils in 1833 and transformed it into one of the leading *grandes marques*.

LEFT The Louis Roederer cellars in Reims.

FAR LEFT Frédéric Rouzaud, the seventh generation of the Roederer dynasty, took over from his father in 2006.

the Czar in 1876. The Russians liked their champagnes sweeter than Coke, which contains 106g/litre of sugar.

Cristal was named after the clear Baccarat crystal, chosen to make the bottle stand out when wrapped in linen at imperial banquets. There was also no punt – the deep indentation at the bottom of a bottle – lest anyone attempt to conceal a grenade. The Czar's paranoia was jusrified: he was assassinated in 1881 after numerous attempts. Roederer remained the official champagne of the imperial court, and Russian sales accounted for a third of production until the Revolution in 1917. It seems there were hefty unpaid bills, which strangely enough the Bolsheviks never settled.

Cristal, no longer in Baccarat crystal because it proved too weak but still with its flat bottom, was relaunched in 1924. With America lost to Prohibition and then the Depression, Louis Roederer was almost bankrupt by the early 1930s, when Camille Olry-Roederer inherited from her late husband. The House was haemorrhaging money thanks to her brother-in-law, who was living like the Sun King as though the Russian Revolution had never happened. So she sacked him. "Imagine the scandal!" says Rouzard. "A woman! Who in those days didn't even have the vote."

The story of Cristal moved on from Russian Czars to rap stars and an unfortunate spat with Jay-Z. The rapper took offence at a comment by Rouzard in 2006, and began dissing his once favourite champagne in favour of gold-plated bottles of Armand de Brignac 'Ace of Spades', which he now happens to own. Demand for Cristal was undented, unlike during the financial crash that followed. Today the wine comes from almost entirely biodynamic vineyards and is given a modest dosage of 9g/litre to allow Roederer to fulfil its simple pledge: "to extract the magic of the Grand Cru", in Rouzard's words.

TASTING NOTES

LOUIS ROEDERER BRUT PREMIER NV

It may not be Cristal, but Roederer's standard bottling sets the bar high with its fine-boned structure, succulent fruit and gossamer-like *mousse*. Over half the grapes are estate-grown and the wine is an equal blend of pinot noir and chardonnay, plus 20% meunier. On the nose there's the faintest trace of nutmeg.

LOUIS ROEDERER ROSÉ 2010

This vintage rosé is two-thirds pinot noir from Grand Cru villages like Cumières, blended with one-third chardonnay from the Côte des Blancs. There is something beautifully tender in the pure, almost austere red fruit, softened by the scent of almonds and French *pâtisserie* and an elegant *mousse* of the finest of bubbles.

ABOVE Louis Roederer Cristal – the world's first prestige *cuvée* – created for Czar Alexander II in the 1870s as an exclusive champagne for the Imperial Russian court. It was later relaunched to a wider audience in 1924.

LEFT Through the careful accumulation of vineyards, Roederer now owns 240 hectares of Champagne, which accounts for around two thirds of its needs.

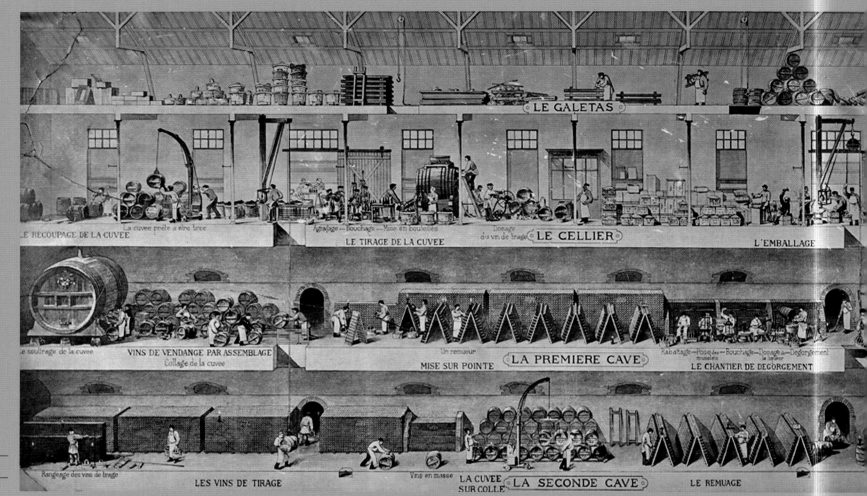

LE GALETAS

LE RECOUPAGE DE LA CUVÉE   La cuvée prête à être tirée   Agrafage – Bouchage – Mise en bouteilles   Dosage du vin de tirage   LE CELLIER   L'EMBALLAGE

LE TIRAGE DE LA CUVÉE

Le soutirage de la cuvée   VINS DE VENDANGE PAR ASSEMBLAGE   Un remueur   RABATTAGE – POSAGE – BOUCHAGE – DOSAGE – DÉGORGEMENT

Collage de la cuvée   MISE SUR POINTE   LA PREMIÈRE CAVE   LE CHANTIER DE DÉGORGEMENT

Rangement des vins de tirage   Vins en masse   LA CUVÉE SUR COLLE   LA SECONDE CAVE   LE REMUAGE

LES VINS DE TIRAGE

ABOVE Everything under one roof at Roederer – from the bags of corks under the eaves to the vats of reserve wine deep in the cellar.

RIGHT Exporting champagne from the region to Russia was not easy. This 1872 steamship shipping note from Antwerp (Anvers in French) to St Petersburg meant that the 3,600 bottles had to be transported by road to the Belgian port before the sea crossing.

SERVICE RÉGULIER PAR STEAMERS

ENTRE

ANVERS, CRONSTADT ET SAINT-PÉTERSBOURG

& VICE-VERSA

SOCIÉTÉ BELGE DE NAVIGATION À VAPEUR

A ANVERS

Directeur-Gérant : Mr F. MOENS

Agents-Généraux à Anvers, Alex. Smyers & Cᵒ

Agents à St-Pétersbourg, Semenoff & Cᵒ

Agent à Liége, Louis RASKIN

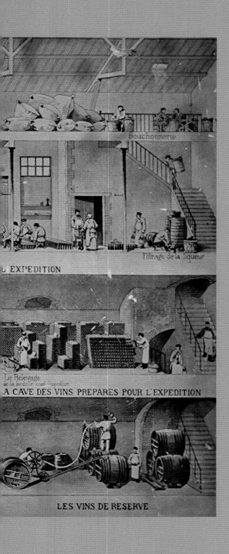

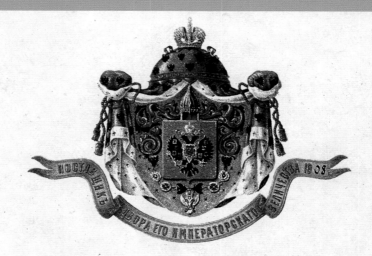

УДОСТОВѢРЕНІЕ.

Канцелярія Министерства Императорскаго Двора симъ свидѣтельствуетъ, что съ Высочайшаго соизволенія, послѣдовавшаго „12" Апрѣля 1908 г. предоставлено владѣльцу торговаго дома въ Реймсѣ „Louis Roederer" _L. Olry Roederer_ званіе поставщика Двора Его Императорскаго Величества, съ правомъ имѣть на вывѣскѣ находящееся на семъ удостовѣреніи изображеніе Малаго Государственнаго герба, съ надписью внизу „Поставщикъ Двора Его Императорскаго Величества. — 1908 года".

С. Петербургъ „13." Апрѣля 1908 года.

Начальникъ Канцеляріи Министерства Свиты Его Величества Генералъ-Маіоръ

Дѣлопроизводитель

№ 4048

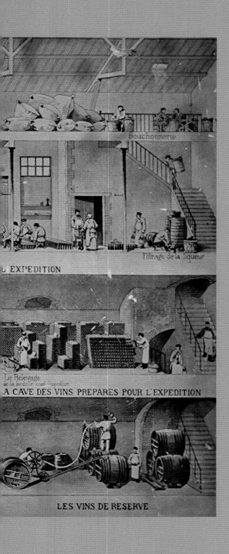

RIGHT The warrant issued by Tsar Nicholas II to Louis Roederer in 1905. The Champagne House had first created Cristal specifically for the Imperial Court of Russia in 1876, and the drink, known as 'Champagne of the Czars', would become available for general consumption only after the 1917 Russian Revolution and the overthrow of the royal family.

RUINART
REIMS

MAISON RUINART IS THE OLDEST ACTIVE CHAMPAGNE HOUSE. IT REMAINED IN FAMILY HANDS FOR OVER TWO CENTURIES UNTIL BOUGHT OUT BY MOËT & CHANDON IN 1963. PERHAPS BETTER KNOWN IN FRANCE THAN ELSEWHERE, IT IS A WELL-RESPECTED HOUSE FAMED FOR THE SEAMLESS PURITY OF ITS RUINART BLANC DES BLANCS.

In the early eighteenth century sparkling champagne was restricted by the ban on transporting wine in bottles. Of course, this did not stop the English adding some sugar to the casks they imported to provoke a secondary fermentation and a few bubbles. But as far as the French are concerned, the story begins in 1728, when the ban on bottled wine was lifted by royal decree.

Nicolas Ruinart, a draper from Reims, wasted no time in setting up the first Champagne House in 1729. Initially it was just a sideline and he used to give bottles away as gifts to his textile clients, but within six years it became his main business, and by 1760 he was selling 36,000 bottles a year. The inspiration had been his uncle, Dom Ruinart, a Benedictine monk who had studied at the Abbey of Saint-Germain-des-Prés near Paris. Apparently, having observed the Parisian courtiers enjoying this new vice, he convinced his nephew that there was money to be had from 'wine with bubbles'.

His fellow Champenois took almost a century to be convinced and even then a few diehards refused to sparkle. Yet from champagne's magnificent debut in art, in Jean-François de Troy's *Le Déjeuner d'huîtres* (The Oyster Lunch, *see* page 27), it's clear there were some early adopters. The bottle on the table was undeniably sparkling – in fact, a true *saut-bouchon* (cork-jumper) if you study the painting carefully.

Frédéric Panaiotis, the current *chef de cave*, would like to think they were drinking Ruinart, being one of only two Houses in existence by the time of the painting in 1735. If the other – Chanoine – has evidence to the contrary he would love to hear from them. Ruinart was the first to invest in Gallo-Roman chalk cellars, and now has 8km of tunnels beneath Reims. It was also the pioneer of rosé champagne way back in 1764. Yet Panaiotis is keen not to be trapped by the past. "Being the oldest means we have to keep being modern," he says. "You have to re-create history."

LEFT A statue of the scholarly Benedictine monk Dom Ruinart, who inspired his nephew to believe that there was a bright future in 'wine with bubbles'.

TASTING NOTES

RUINART BLANC DE BLANCS NV

The House likes to claim that chardonnay is "the very soul of Ruinart", and this is certainly one of the top NV Blanc de Blancs with its racy acidity and peach and pear flavours. There's an almost fleshy character, perhaps from the Montagne de Reim's grapes, and a trace of chalk and wet stones.

DOM RUINART BLANC DE BLANCS 2004

Perhaps not as famous as that other "Dom", but Ruinart's *prestige cuvée* made entirely of Grand Cru chardonnay, two-thirds from the Côtes des Blancs, is a real delight. There are spring flowers and marzipan on the nose, a vibrant core of citrus fruit and a long tapering, mineral finish.

If he could, he would ask the Ruinart family who ran the House for over two centuries why they never invested more in vineyards, especially before the First World War when land was cheap. As he says, some champagne villages refused to be classified in 1910 because there was more money in cereals than grapes. The family did own 17 hectares, but it seems they kept them when Moët & Chandon bought the House in 1963.

André Ruinart was one of the first merchants to embrace modern art, commissioning the Czech artist Alphonse Mucha in 1896 to paint a series of posters for the champagne. They featured a beautiful, near-life-size woman with wild, coiling locks of hair and a champagne *coupe* held aloft issuing a profusion of star-like bubbles. With the clue in the name, the artistic connection has been maintained and today Ruinart is a major sponsor of art fairs around the world from San Francisco to Kyoto.

In 1919 André Ruinart died, leaving his young, English wife, Mary Kate Charlotte Riboldi, Viscountess Ruinart de Brimont, to try and rebuild the House after the devastation of war. She was from a humble background, and had been orphaned at an early age. Aside from the almost complete flattening of Reims under the German artillery, Ruinart had lost one important market after the Russian Revolution, and was about to lose another a year later. The US Congress had just ratified the Volstead Act, which led to Prohibition in January 1920.

For the next five years Viscountess Charlotte helped keep Ruinart afloat until her son was old enough to take over. Today Ruinart has access to some wonderful grapes, especially grand cru chardonnay from the Montagne de Reims.

Panaiotis insists Ruinart has a clear identity. "We're the house of chardonnay," he says, describing the house style as one of "aromatic freshness". It certainly deserves to be better known.

ABOVE Tunnels were dug into the soft chalk beneath Champagne during the time of the Romans, who used the material for building. Ruinart was the first House to use the tunnels as cellars.

LEFT The first established Champagne House was founded by Nicolas Ruinart, a draper from Reims, in 1729.

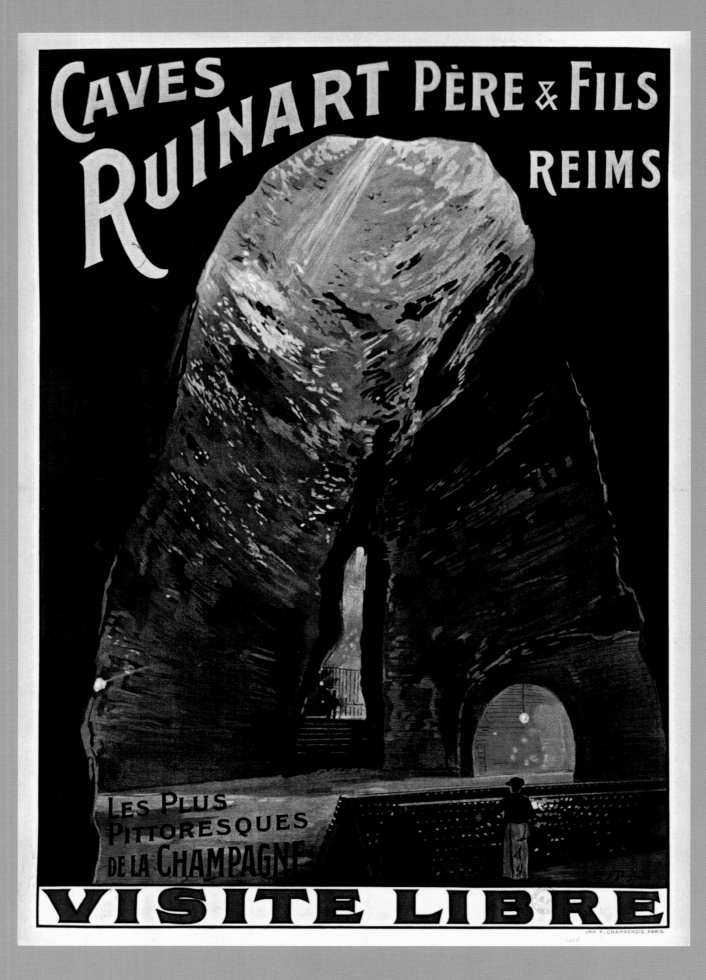

OPPOSITE Painted by Louis Tauzin in 1914, just before the First World War, the poster proclaims Ruinart's cellars to be "the most picturesque in Champagne".

LEFT The Czech painter Alphonse Mucha's famous Art Deco poster for the brand (c.1898).

TAITTINGER
REIMS

FROM AN ALMOST STANDING START IN THE DARK DAYS OF THE 1930s, TAITTINGER HAS RISEN TO BECOME THE SIXTH-LARGEST CHAMPAGNE HOUSE WITH ANNUAL SALES PUSHING SIX MILLION BOTTLES. WITHIN THE CORPORATE WORLD OF CHAMPAGNE, ITS BOSS IS AS REFRESHING AS HIS SENSUAL, CHARDONNAY-BASED WINES.

"Sex has played a huge role in the success of champagne. You can trace it back to the mistresses of Louis XIV," declared the president of Champagne Taittinger in an interview with *Decanter* magazine in 2014. "I constantly tell my colleagues that champagne is a symbol of pleasure, joie de vivre, seduction and sex. Surely that's something we should celebrate?"

Amid the corporate suits in Champagne, Pierre-Emmanuel Taittinger is a real breath of fresh air – a man full of passion, warmth and wit. He joined the family firm in 1976, 44 years after his grandfather founded the House. Pierre Taittinger had been billeted at the Château de la Marquetterie near Épernay as a young officer during the First World War.

After the war he decided to buy the Château and its few hectares of vineyards, followed by the acquisition of Champagne Fourneaux, founded in 1743, which he eventually rechristened Taittinger. The family also bought and restored the home of the Counts of Champagne in Reims, and moved in in 1933. And it acquired the thirteenth-century cellars of the St Niçaise Abbey, where its *Comtes de Champagne cuvée* is aged.

Before and after the Second World War, Pierre and his sons, Jean and François, embarked on a great vineyard-buying spree. "It was very much a strategic decision," says Pierre-Emmanuel's son, Clovis Taittinger, who believes that if the two brothers had lived longer they might have acquired 800 hectares or more. Still, it was a good time to buy when prices were nothing compared to the €1 million or so charged for a hectare of decent vineyards today, and Taittinger now has 250 hectares. Around 70 are in the Aube, where they began buying up good-quality sites for chardonnay and pinot noir in the 1960s, long before most of their rivals.

By this stage Claude Taittinger was in charge. "It was Claude who developed the revolutionary style that was fresh and elegant," says Clovis. "At the time champagne was very much pinot-driven and used old-style *barriques*, while Taittinger was sophisticated, feminine and chardonnay-based. It was without wood, without make-up

ABOVE Pierre-Emmanuel Taittinger, current chairman and grandson of the founder, Pierre Taittinger. He joined the business in 1976, but did not take over from his uncle as chairman until 1998.

LEFT Neat, corrugated slopes belonging Taittinger, and part of the extensive 250 hectares of vineyards the House has accumulated since the 1920s.

ABOVE The House owns thirteenth-century wine cellars beneath the St Niçaise Abbey that are now a Unesco World Heritage site. It is in here that the famous *Comtes de Champagne* cuvée has been aged since the 1960s.

and very sexy." His father once caused a frisson in the land of the draconian, anti-alcohol *Loi Évin*, by claiming that champagne's stiffest competition came not from other sparkling wines but from Viagra.

The pinnacle of Taittinger's faith in chardonnay is found in its *Comtes de Champagne* Blanc de Blancs, a vintage blend from six or seven top villages like Avize, Cramant and Le Mesnil-sur-Oger which was first released in 1952. A soupçon of spice and creamy texture is added from 5% of the wine being matured in new oak, and the whole is aged for 10 years in the cellar. A *Comtes de Champagne* rosé was added in 1966, and this contains 70% pinot noir from prime sites in the Montaigne de Reims.

The extended family had been growing the group to include prestigious hotels, like the Crillon in Paris, a perfume house and Baccarat Crystal. With this added financial muscle and its base of vineyards, Taittinger's position seemed to be rock-solid when Pierre-Emanuel took over from his uncle Claude in 1998. But cracks were opening up beneath the surface and, when an American hotel chain bid for the group in 2005, six of the seven branches of the family voted "yes". But the Americans didn't want the champagne, and soon it was back on the market. Somehow with help from the local Crédit Agricole, Pierre-Emmanuel beat off 10 global bids and managed to buy back Taittinger for €660 million in May 2006. To celebrate he claims to have shared a bottles of *Comtes de Champagne* with his wife and daughter, and danced round the dining-room table in his underpants.

Clovis denies the last part, perhaps blocking out memories of an embarrassing dad, but either way the news went down well in Champagne. So is this family-owned House finally safe? "Well, we've just had five of our best years ever," says Clovis. "The passion's still there. The ambition's still there, but we'll never take it for granted."

ABOVE A tall, mermaid-like Grace Kelly shows off her curves for Comtes de Champagne – Taittinger's top-of-the-range *Blanc de Blancs* launched in 1952.

TASTING NOTES

TAITTINGER BRUT RÉSERVE NV

There's a breezy lightness of being in this chardonnay-led blend that makes it such a fine apéritif champagne. With fruit from *cru* villages in the Côte des Blancs blended with pinot noir from the Aube, there is a delicate scent of acacia and lemon sherbet. On the tongue – lemon zest and a creamy, vivacious *mousse*.

TAITTINGER COMTES DE CHAMPAGNE BLANC DE BLANCS 2004

It is worth taking a moment to appreciate the complex aromas of Comtes de Champagne. There are white flowers, peach blossom, orange zest and wet pebbles. Then taste the refreshing, clean-cut flavours of lemon and cranberries, held tight by a coiled-up acidity that will gradually unfurl over time.

LEFT The Château de la Marquetterie, near Épernay, so called for its patchwork vineyards of black and white grapes, was briefly home to a young Pierre Taittinger during the First World War.

VEUVE CLICQUOT

REIMS

IN THE SPACE OF A GENERATION THE WIDOWED MADAME CLICQUOT TOOK A SMALL CHAMPAGNE HOUSE IN REIMS IN 1805 AND PROPELLED IT TO STARDOM. NOW PART OF THE LUXURY BRAND EMPIRE LVMH, VEUVE CLICQUOT CONTINUES TO LIVE UP TO HER LEGACY 150 YEARS AFTER HER DEATH.

Widowed at 27 with a three-year-old daughter and a business to run, Barbe Nicole Clicquot Ponsardin has a story reads like a film script. One can picture Julia Roberts playing the part of the plucky single mum who, in a man's world and against all odds, builds one of the most powerful champagne brands of all time. Back at the dawn of the nineteenth century when the tale begins, however, the key point was not 'single mum', but 'widow'.

The House was founded in 1772 by Philippe Clicquot, whose son François-Marie built up sales to 60,000 bottles by 1804. A comfortable life beckoned for Barbe Nicole, his well-connected wife, whose father was a wealthy textile merchant and mayor of Reims. But François-Marie died a year later, leaving his widowed bride the chance to shine as one of the great champagne entrepreneurs. With Europe at war and the English navy blockading the seas, trade links to exciting new markets among the Baltic States and beyond were cut off. Things looked bleak, and as her devoted salesman, Louis Bohn, wrote: "Business is terribly stagnant … prices are plummeting."

Then, streaking high above the vineyards, came the Great Comet of 1811, which Barbe Nicole took as an omen for an exceptional vintage. She was determined that her wine's newfound Russian admirers should not be denied despite the Czar's boycott of French wines in 1812. A Dutch ship was chartered with instructions to carry no other champagne but 10,550 bottles of Veuve Clicquot to the Baltic port of Königsberg. Without waiting to hear news, the canny widow dispatched another 12,000 a week later.

You are "the terror of all your competitors", wrote an ecstatic Louis Bohn as he described the Russians "with their tongues hanging out" to taste the Comet vintage. Soon he was boasting of Veuve Clicquot's spring-like clarity thanks to *chef de cave* Antoine-Aloys Müller, who had perfected the technique of *remuage* (the removal of the yeasty sediment) by riddling the bottles in a specially made *pupitre*. Whether or not he actually drilled holes in Barbe Nicole's desk to make the device, she was

BELOW Veuve Clicquot's palatial headquarters in Reims, a testament to the ruthless determination of its namesake and the success of her brand in nineteenth-century Russia.

thrilled and tried hard to keep it a secret.

She failed in that, but she did succeed, unlike Napoleon, in conquering Russia, which became champagne's second-biggest export market after Britain, and helped propel Veuve Clicquot's sales to more than 400,000 bottles by 1850. That year, sensing that her daughter and son-in-law, the Comte de Chevigné, wouldn't be able to cope, she handed the business to her partner, Edouard Werlé. (The Comte de Chevigné had discovered a wonderful way of extracting money from his wealthy mother-in-law to pay off his gambling debts.)

Veuve Clicquot died in 1866, but the brand lived on under Werlé and his descendants. Sales had topped three million bottles by 1900 thanks to Russia and growing success in the United States. That number has since soared to an estimated 18 million bottles, of which around 15 million is the famous egg-yolk 'Yellow Label' trademarked in 1877. The colour is defended with litigious zeal lest anyone come close to Pantone 137C. An exception is made for Glenmorangie Single Malt, for that too is owned by LVMH following its acquisition of Veuve Clicquot in 1986.

A year later, Veuve Clicquot released its first *prestige cuvée* – La Grande Dame, in tribute to the widow herself. Two-thirds pinot noir, it comes from eight special Grand Cru sites in Aÿ, Verzenay, Ambonnay and Bouzy, from within the House's 393 hectares that supply one-fifth of its needs.

The 'Yellow Label' has become drier with a *dosage* down from 12g to 9g/litre, a fraction of the sugary 150g Veuve Clicquot once guzzled by the Romanovs. Yet bridging the gap is the new Veuve Clicquot Rich with 60g/l of sugar in a glitzy silver bottle. Its sweetness is designed for drinking over ice and with one added garnish, for a younger generation, perhaps weaned on Prosecco.

TASTING NOTES

VEUVE CLICQUOT BRUT NV

The world-famous "Yellow Label" and centrepiece of the Veuve Clicquot collection has instantly recognisable flavour, power and consistency. It is a reliable crowd-pleaser with its supple texture and red-apple crunch of acidity, which gains complexity if you lay it down for a few years.

VEUVE CLICQUOT VINTAGE 2008

Two-thirds pinot noir, one-third chardonnay and a spoonful of pinot meunier make up this youthful vintage expression with its 8g/l *dosage*. There is a steely core to the bright, elegant stone fruit flavours, and a lingering mineral note, but it needs time to unwind a little.

TOP A magazine advertisement from the 1930s, promoting the distinctly orange 'Yellow Label' of the flagship brand, whose sales are now estimated at around 15 million bottles a year.

LEFT The original champagne widow – the indefatigable Barbe Nicole Clicquot Ponsardin, who took over her husband's small yet thriving champagne business in 1805.

FAR LEFT This staircase, descending to Clicquot's cellars, is marked with all of the Champagne House's declared vintage years.

BEHIND THE BUBBLES

OF COURSE THE CHAMPAGNE TRADE IS INFINITELY LARGER AND MORE COMPLEX THAN THE PREVIOUS PAGES MIGHT SUGGEST. THERE ARE PLENTY MORE FAMOUS BRANDS, OR *GRANDES MARQUES*, TO CONSIDER, PLUS A NUMBER OF POPULAR CHAMPAGNES LIKE JACQUART AND NICOLAS FEUILLATTE, PRODUCED BY THE CO-OPERATIVES, AND AN ALMOST ENDLESS SEA OF GROWER CHAMPAGNES.

To help navigate our way through champagne, it is worth considering the structure of the trade and how it has evolved. Today there are some 15,800 growers who own 90% of the 34,000 hectares of vineyards within the *appellation*. None of the major Champagne Houses is self-sufficient in grapes, and while some like Roederer and Bollinger own two-thirds of their needs, some have no vineyards at all. The Houses, of which there are around 300, own just over 3,100 hectares between them, yet they sell two thirds of all champagne and 90% of exports.

In 1882 the *Syndicat du Commerce des Vins de Champagne* was established to defend the wine and its geographic roots. At the time the name 'champagne' risked becoming as generic as *eau de Cologne* with producers outside the region happily using the c-word. Membership of the *Syndicat* was theoretically open to any *négociant*, or champagne merchant in the Marne, and basically included anyone of any standing in the trade. Eventually, in 1964, an elite emerged, calling itself the *Syndicat des Grandes Marques de Champagne*. Among the original 25 grandees on the list were Bollinger, Krug, Perrier-Jouët and Louis Roederer. Another five, including Canard-Duchêne and Gosset, were added later. As with the Royal Enclosure during Royal Ascot's horse race meeting, admission was strictly by invitation only.

This self-appointed champagne aristocracy was officially disbanded in 1997, because its members were unable to agree a sort of quality criteria on which they could base their alleged superiority. However, the term *grande marque* lives on as a reference to the big, traditional brands. The relationship between the growers in Champagne and the Champagne Houses who control the market, particularly abroad, has always been complicated. On their own, individual growers, with less than two hectares of vines between them on average, appear powerless compared with the big brand-owners. But, collectively, the growers clearly have strength in numbers, and this is what inspired them to form co-operatives to obtain the greatest value for their key asset – the grapes.

The co-operatives, whose membership can run to thousands of growers, play a key role as middlemen between the big Houses and the growers. It allows the major groups, whose vineyards supply less than they need to meet production targets, to buy a large quantity of grapes or *vin clair* (base wine) in one go. The alternative would be a time-consuming nightmare of thousands of contracts with the individual growers. The advantage for the grower is that his or her co-operative can use its muscle to obtain the best price for the grapes. Top-rated vineyards were recently earning up to €6 per kilo, of which you need 1.2kg per 75cl bottle, or 1.5kg if you are using just the first pressing of grapes.

The strongest co-operatives have developed their own brands in direct competition to the established names. Nicolas Feuillate, owned by the region's biggest co-operative with 5,000 members, has become a Top Five champagne brand. If it grows much bigger, some of the Houses who rely on the co-operative for fruit may go thirsty. Meanwhile, among the thousands of growers, few have not at some stage dreamed of making their own champagne, rather than simply selling their grapes or *vin clair* to others. In lean times, with plummeting demand for their fruit, it was not so much a dream as a dire necessity to make wine. The growers had to do something with their leftover grapes. In good times, with grape prices far higher than in other wine regions, you would imagine there would be much less incentive.

Then again, if others are surfing a great surge in demand for champagne and reaping the rewards, why not join in if you have sufficient vineyards in the right place and the balls to give it a try? The up-front costs in equipment and having to tie up money in stock is an obvious barrier to entry, and while making wine is relatively straightforward, selling it is anything but. Then again, in this new digital age, it has become a lot easier to gain recognition, and, as countless craft brewers and boutique distillers have proved, there is plenty of antipathy towards big brands these days. With their *terroir*-driven approach, some grower champagnes have achieved cult status among top sommeliers and on the blogosphere.

OPPOSITE The balance of power in Champagne lies between the big brands who dominate the market, particularly abroad, and the growers who own 90% of the vineyards. Today more than 2,000 growers produce their own wine under their own label.

BELOW Within 40 years of its launch, Nicolas Feuillate has become a massive, 10-million-bottle brand. Owned by the region's biggest co-operative, it poses a direct challenge to the long-established grandees of Champagne.

OTHER FAMOUS CHAMPAGNE HOUSES

THERE ARE PLENTY MORE CHAMPAGNE HOUSES TO CONSIDER, RANGING FROM THE BOUTIQUE END OF THE SPECTRUM TO BIG NAMES THAT HAVE SUFFERED IN THE CONSOLIDATION AMONG THE KEY BRAND OWNERS. SOME HAVE EMERGED, STRIPPED OF THEIR VINEYARDS, YET DETERMINED TO RECLAIM THEIR REPUTATION UNDER NEW OWNERSHIP.

While other champagnes competed to supply the courts and principalities of Europe, **Mercier** was aimed at the burgeoning middle classes, particularly in France. Eugène Mercier grouped together five small Champagne Houses in 1858, and then created his own brand. He built a large, functional winery with direct access to the railways in 1871, and two decades later took the Paris Exhibition by storm with his most famous publicity stunt. This was the 'world's biggest blending vat' that took seven years to build and was towed from Épernay to Paris by 24 white oxen. Ever since then it has been one of the biggest-selling champagnes in France, a market that accounts for around 80% of its sales. The House accumulated 220 hectares of vineyards, with the most planted variety being pinot meunier. This is said to explain the soft, youthful, easy-drinking style of Mercier Brut NV. In 1970 Moët & Chandon bought the brand, and to some extent treated it as a *sous marque*, or second label, even though it still comfortably outsells

Moët in the domestic market.

Eight years after Mercier was swallowed up by what is now LVMH, Veuve Clicquot did the same to **Canard-Duchêne**. The House was founded in the village of Ludes on the northern flank of the Montagne de Reims in 1868 after the marriage of a cooper called Victor Canard and Léonie Duchêne, whose family were growers. The grand crest on the label came from the Imperial Russian Court once supplied by the House. A century later it was on semi- permanent special offer in French supermarkets where many of the two million-plus bottles were sold.

In 2003 the House was bought, and some might say rescued, by Alain Thiénot, a former champagne broker, who had been quietly building up his own champagne empire since 1981. With Canard-Duchêne he became a much bigger player, but his new purchase was clearly in need of some TLC. Cellar master Laurent Fédou has freshened up the house style, while the large, somewhat industrial-

ABOVE Eugène Mercier, who founded Mercier in 1858, aged just 20, built it into one of the most powerful champagne brands of all.

LEFT Mercier currently owns 220 hectares of vineyards within its LVMH stable, the most planted grape variety being pinot meunier.

ABOVE The cellars of Canard-Duchêne were once owned by LVMH, but it was bought out by Alain Thiénot in 2003.

looking cellars in Ludes have been much improved. Meanwhile the group has been building its own brand: Champagne Thiénot, launched in 1985 and also made by Fédou.

Another large House, is that of **G.H Martel**, based in Épernay and founded a year after Canard-Duchêne in 1869. It was really developed by André Tabourin from the 1920s until his death in 1979, when the firm was sold to Ernest Rapeneau, whose family also own Charles de Cazenove champagne. Today the firm is run by his grandson Christophe. He is also the winemaker, while his older brother Jean-François handles sales and marketing. Martel owns some 200 hectares of vineyards planted with mainly chardonnay and pinot noir, which supplies around one-fifth of its needs. Martel is probably better known in France than in the UK or the United States, and is often on offer in the supermarkets. In 1989 it decided to launch a well-regarded good value *prestige cuvée* called *Cuvée Victoire*.

Up in the Montagne de Reims in the village of Chigny-les-Roses – as floral as it sounds – the **Cattier** family have been growers since the eighteenth century, finally becoming producers after the First World War. Today they own around 35 hectares, mainly in premier cru vineyards in Chigny-les-Roses, Rilly-la-Montagne, Taissy and Ludes, with half given over to pinot noir. Cattier's pride and joy is a tiny walled plot within the commune of 2.2 hectares called Clos du Moulin from where they make their *prestige cuvée*. Like Taittinger's *Comtes de Champagne*, it is always a blend of three vintages. They also make a Blanc des Blancs from the Montagne, which makes for an interesting contrast to the classic Côtes des Blancs style of chardonnay.

In 2000 Cattier set out to create the world's most expensive champagne – **Armand de Brignac** – in a gold-plated bottle. Having launched it six years later, the so-called Ace of Spades quickly hit the headlines thanks to the rapper Jay Z (Shawn Carter) spotting it glinting in his local New York wine shop. Within no time he was rapping about "this Spade shit", around the time he was dissing Louis Roederer's Cristal in 2006. Jay-Z went on to invest in the brand still produced by Cattier and according to the

writer Zack O'Malley Greenburg he personally makes "a little over US$4 million" a year from it. But "is the wine inside worth the hype and not inconsiderable price?' wondered Tyson Stelzer in *The Champagne Guide*. He declared it: "evenly balanced and well made, albeit very young and straightforward" – so by the sound of it, probably not at around £180 a pop.

Considerably more affordable is the highly rated champagne **Bruno Paillard**, founded by the current chairman and CEO of Lanson-BCC – the biggest brand-owner after LVMH. Coming from an ancient family of growers, Paillard learned his trade as a broker. Most of what he sourced disappeared into supermarket own-label champagne, but particularly good parcels were kept aside and sold under his name. Having built a prototype brand, he became the first person in modern times to establish a Champagne House from scratch in 1981. The wines are food-friendly and built to last with pinot noir the lead grape, while the running of this boutique House is largely left to Bruno's daughter Alice.

TOP LEFT   Bruno Paillard, the first man to found a Champagne House in modern times. His House was established in 1981.

TOP   When it comes to bling and big-format bottles no one out-aces Armand de Brignac, whose 30 litre Midas bottles sell in nightclubs for six-figure sums.

ABOVE   Bottles of liquid gold – Armand de Brignac's Ace of Spades champagne, ageing in Salon's cellars in the Côtes des Blancs. In America, the brand is part of rapper Jay Z's business empire.

Heading south from the Montagne de Reims you hit the ancient champagne village of Aÿ. It was here that William Deutz worked for Bollinger before setting up his own House next-door in 1838. Champagne **Deutz** suffered in the riots of 1911 when its cellar was destroyed, but survived in family hands until the early 1990s when Louis Roederer bought it. Today Deutz owns 42 of the 200 hectares of *premier* and *grand cru* vineyards it sources grapes from, all in the Marne valley and within 20 miles of Aÿ. Its new owners have more than trebled production to more than two million bottles, yet under the dynamic leadership of Roederer's Fabrice Rosset, the champagne's reputation seems as high as ever.

The riots also claimed Château d'Aÿ, which was burnt to the ground only to be rebuilt two years later. The original château was a wedding gift to Edmond de Ayala, a Colombian diplomat, from his father-in-law the Viscount of Mareuil, along with some esteemed vineyards. Champagne **Ayala** was founded soon after, in 1860, and later became the favourite fizz of King George VI. Its reputation had all but collapsed by 2005 when rescued by its neighbour, Bollinger. Under its new owners the focus has been on Ayala's bone-dry house style, notably its crisp, sugar-free Brut Nature. There is also a well-regarded Blanc des Blancs and a *prestige cuvée* called Perle d'Ayala.

The Swiss de Venoge family was linked to the neighbouring village of Dizy before Henri-Marc de Venoge returned from Switzerland with his Italian wife to found Champagne **De Venoge** in 1837. While his son Joseph helped develop the business in France and Belgium, his other son Léon did the same in the US having emigrated there. De Venoge launched its Cordon Bleu brand in 1851, some 25 years before Mumm's rather more famous Cordon Rouge hit the shelves. By then third-generation Gaëtan de Venoge had been one of the founders of the *Sydicat des Grandes Marques*. Over time the family connection petered out and the House eventually became part of the Lanson-BCC group. In 2014 it was announced that it would be moving into Maison Gallice, one of the grandest houses in Épernay's Avenue de Champagne.

Four years before Maison Gallice was built in 1899, the Viscount Florens de Castellane launched his champagne house. With its St Andrew's cross in bold red, Champagne **De Castellane** sought to stand out from rivals with a mere single sash like Mumm and De Venoge on their label. And its HQ towered above its rivals in Épernay with its striped brick tower that still offers a commanding view of the town. Today De Castellane is part of the Laurent-Perrier empire.

One other champagne house to mention in Épernay is **Alfred Gratien**, founded in 1867 by a man who believed "champagne should be to wine what haute couture is to fashion". His descendants eventually sold out to Henkell & Söhnlein in 2004, which caused some alarm going from family-ownership to that of Germany's biggest Sekt producer. However Nicolas Jaeger was retained as *chef de cave* and as the fourth generation of his family to hold the post, there is a great sense of continuity at Alfred Gratien. The firm have been supplying the Wine Society with their well-regarded house champagne since 1906.

Heading south on the D10 from Épernay you pass through Cuis, Cramant, Avize and the other famous villages of the Côtes des Blancs. The fact this is chardonnay country is epitomised by the boutique house of **Salon**. Aimé Salon released the first bottles in 1911 with the sole purpose of expressing this one grape variety from a single grand cru village, Le Mesnil-sur-Oger, from a particular vintage with no blending involved. The House itself was founded after the First World, and has been releasing its vintage wines four or five times a decade on average. It was the legendary '28 Salon that Bernard de Nonacourt discovered as a young tank commander in Hitler's secret cellar in a cave in the Bavarian Alps in 1945. After the war, de Nonancourt took over Laurent-Perrier and finally

BELOW Set up by William Deutz in the village of Aÿ in 1838, Champagne Deutz is now owned by Louis Roederer.

BOTTOM LEFT Founded by a Colombian diplomat in 1860, Ayala had a reputation in need of considerable TLC when rescued by the neighbouring House of Bollinger in 2005.

BOTTOM RIGHT Drappier is one of the few producers who still grow the rare champagne grape, petit meslier of its Quattuor blend that also features pinot blanc, arbane and chardonnay.

bought Salon in 1999. Laurent-Perrier also acquired Salon's stable-mate and fellow chardonnay devotee, Champagne **Delamotte**, the fifth oldest Champagne House, founded in 1760 in Le Mesnil.

At the southern end of the Côtes des Blancs is the premier cru village of Vertus, home to **Duval-Leroy**. From the sight of its futuristic, solar-panelled winery you would never guess the House was founded back in 1859. It is still in family hands, under the redoubtable Carol Duval-Leroy, who became a modern-day champagne widow on the death of her husband Jean Charles in 1991, aged just 39. Duval-Leroy controls 200 hectares of vineyards, mainly in Vertus and mainly planted with chardonnay, and in keeping with those solar panels is firmly committed to sustainable viticulture. It was the first House to produce a *cuvée* from organically-grown grapes, and since 2000 has halved its use of herbicides. Today it buys in around 80% of its grapes to produce 5.5 million bottles a year. Its chardonnay-led top *cuvée* – Femme de Champagne is only released in the best years.

As you head down to the Côte des Bar, chardonnay gives way to pinot noir thanks to the pioneering work of men like Georges Collot of **Drappier**, who was dubbed *père pinot* (father pinot) for his efforts to replace the discredited gamay grape that once dominated the vineyards. One of Drappier's pure pinot noir champagnes was the favourite of Charles de Gaulle when he retired to the nearby village of Colombey-les-Deux-Églises. Today Georges' grandson Michel Drappier heads up the House that owns 55 hectares and has control of a further 50, making it the most important producer in the region. Drappier has been based in Urville since 1803 and ages its champagne in the magnificent vaulted cellars of the 12th-century Clairvaux Abbey. Its flagship wine is Carte d'Or, which is at least 80% pinot noir, while its top expression is the single vineyard Grande Sendrée that also comes as a rosé.

LEFT Champagne De Castellane's elaborate brick tower is a prominent landmark in Épernay.

MIDDLE LEFT Since Carol Duval-Leroy took over the family house in 1991, annual production has grown to 5.5 million bottles.

BOTTOM LEFT Champagne De Venoge was founded in 1837 by Henri-Marc de Venoge from Switzerland. Today it is part of the Lanson-BCC group.

BELOW Salon only produces Blanc de Blancs champagne in Mesnil-sur-Oger. Bernard de Nonancourt discovered it in Hitler's secret wine cellar in 1945, and eventually bought the boutique House 54 years later.

FOLLOWING PAGES The sun breaks through the clouds over the patchwork vineyards of the Vallée de la Marne.

CHAMPAGNE CO-OPERATIVES

THE IDEA OF THE LOCAL CO-OPERATIVE WINERY CRUSHING THE GRAPES OF ALL ITS GROWERS, FERMENTING THE JUICE IN A GIANT STAINLESS-STEEL TANK AND BOTTLING THE RESULT, DOESN'T NECESSARILY SUGGEST QUALITY. ALL OVER EUROPE, AND PROBABLY IN THIS REGION AS WELL, THERE ARE CO-OPERATIVES WHERE THERE IS NO REAL ATTEMPT TO BE SELECTIVE IN THE BLIND PURSUIT OF VOLUME. YET, IN CHAMPAGNE, THERE ARE A SURPRISING NUMBER OF REALLY GOOD CO-OPERATIVES, WHOSE WINEMAKERS APPEAR TO BE EVERY BIT AS PASSIONATE AND SKILLED AS THOSE OF THE *GRANDES MARQUES*. THEIR WINES CONSISTENTLY SHINE IN BLIND TASTINGS, AND STAND OUT ON THE SHELF FOR THEIR RELATIVE GOOD VALUE.

Take **Mailly Grand Cru**, a co-operative set up in 1929 to protect the growers in this leading village on the northern flank of the Montagne de Reims during the Depression. It was established by Gabriel Simon with 24 founding members, and you can gauge their commitment by the fact they began digging out the co-operative's chalk cellars by hand, a task that took 40 years. Today there are more than 70 members who own 74 hectares between them, or one-third of all Mailly's grand cru vineyards. Here on the northern fringes of planet wine, the received wisdom is that you need to blend from a wider area if you want to make good wine every year. But in Mailly, as in the village of Aÿ, it seems there is enough variety in slopes and topography to hedge against vintage variation. With some 500 parcels of mainly top-quality pinot noir, the winemaker has a great spectrum of wines to create the blends.

While Mailly Grand Cru sells 90% of its production under its label, a far more typical scenario for a co-operative is that of Champagne **Palmer**, which sells 70% of its fruit to the Champagne Houses, keeping the best for itself. It was founded by seven growers after the Second World War and now has more than 200 members

with 365 hectares in total spread across 40 villages. The vineyards are mainly grand and premier cru in the Monatgne de Reims. No one quite knows where the English name came from, though it may have been inspired by Huntley & Palmer. Apparently the Champenois considered them the *crème de la crème* of biscuits after the war. Today it is one of the top-rated smaller co-operatives, with annual sales of half a million bottles.

This is dwarfed by **Jacquart**, the flagship brand of the Alliance Group, an amalgam of three big co-operatives, established in 1994, which now has a total of 1,800 members. Jacquart itself dates from the early 1960s with just 30 growers involved at the start. That number has since blossomed to around 700, covering 1,000 hectares in 64 different villages. Today more than three million bottles of Jacquart are produced with strong sales in the UK, the USA and Japan. In the cellar is the talented young winemaker, Floriane Eznack, who joined in 2010 from Veuve Clicquot, while one-third of production is of Jacquart's popular Mosaique Brut NV.

The biggest player in the Côte des Blancs is the Union

BELOW Set up in 1929, the Mailly Grand Cru co-operative now has 74 hectares of vineyards owned and is farmed by 70 members.

Champagne in Avize, with no fewer than 13 co-operatives under its umbrella and a production equivalent to 12 million bottles. Between them the members own 1,200 hectares, nearly all in top-rated villages, mostly planted with chardonnay in the Côte des Blancs, but with some pinot noir in the Montagne de Reims as well. The co-operative sells around 2.5 million bottles under its own labels, principally **De Saint Gall**, which has done well in the UK through Marks & Spencer. The rest is sold off to the likes of Moët & Chandon, Taittinger and Piper Heidsieck. These Houses are prepared to pay top dollar for the best grapes, which might find their way into Dom Pérignon or Taittinger's *Comtes de Champagnes* for example.

Down the road in Le Mesnil-sur-Oger, home to Krug's legendary Clos du Mesnil Blanc de Bancs, is Champagne **Le Mesnil**, a very upmarket co-operative with around 300 hectares of east-facing slopes in this famous grand cru. With a tiny average holding, the 553 members farm their plots like allotments, while the co-operative sells all but 8% of its production to the big Champagne Houses. It sells little more than 120,000 bottles under its own label.

The giant **Nicolas Feuillatte** couldn't be more different. It is the brand of the region's biggest co-operative, with 2,250 hectares owned by its 5,000-plus members. With sales pushing 10 million bottles as of 2013, it claims to be third to Top of the Pops Moët & Chandon and Veuve Clicquot and the best-seller in French supermarkets. The original M. Feuillatte, who died in 2014, made a fortune from the post-war instant coffee boom in the States before buying 12 hectares in Champagne and launching his wine in 1976. He sold it to the co-operative 10 years later, but continued as its brand ambassador, particularly in the USA. Feuillatte's massive, shiny HQ in the village of Chouilly stands in stark contrast to the palatial, *fin de siècle* mansions of the Champagne House in Épernay and Reims. And

there is no attempt to conceal the scale of the operation, with visitors whisked on airport-style conveyor belts past giant vats of gleaming stainless steel.

All this was a far cry from the genteel world of Claude-Joseph Devaux, who found herself widowed and in charge of a Champagne House in Épernay in 1846. No fewer than three widows ran **Champagne Devaux**, the last one dying in 1951, but the name lives on as the highly rated brand of the main co-operative in the Aube. Formerly known as the Union Auboise and run by the dynamic Laurent Gillet, it has 800 growers and 1,384 hectares of primarily pinot noir vineyards.

TOP LEFT The imposing head office of Jacquart, the flagship brand of the giant Alliance Group of cooperatives that now has around 1,800 members.

ABOVE A poster from the 1920s advertising Champagne Devaux, then privately owned, now the brand of the biggest cooperative in the Aube.

BELOW The massive Nicolas Feuillatte has access to no less than 2,250 hectares of vineyards owned by its 5,000 members.

GROWER CHAMPAGNES

WITH MORE THAN 2,000 GROWER PRODUCERS, OR *RÉCOLTANT-MANIPULANTS*, TO CHOOSE FROM, VISITING CHAMPAGNE CAN BE TOTALLY BEWILDERING WITH ITS PROFUSION OF UNKNOWN NAMES. HOW MUCH SIMPLER IS THE UK HIGH STREET, WITH ITS SELECTION OF TRIED AND TESTED BRANDS AND A SCATTERING OF CHEAPER OWN-LABEL ALTERNATIVES. HERE ARE JUST A FEW GROWER CHAMPAGNES, IN ALPHABETICAL ORDER, WORTH LOOKING OUT FOR …

The **Agrapart** family in Avize have been doing it longer than most, and brothers Pascal and Fabrice are fourth-generation grower producers. With 10 hectares in their home village and Oger, Cramant and Oiry, the vineyards are as natural as can be, though not certified organic or biodynamic. The vines are well into middle age, with some pushing 70 years old, and the wines are all aged on their lees for at least three years, seven in the case of vintage bottlings. Pascal Agrapart has been hailed a genius in the cellar, though he shrugs it off, giving credit to the *terroir* and the vagaries of the weather.

To the north in the village of Bouzy, in the Montagne de Reims, you will find **Paul Bara** with a similar holding to that of the Agroparts. The family were growers in Bouzy and supplied the Champagne Houses and then the local co-operative for more than a century, before they began bottling their wines in earnest

after the Second World War. Old vine pinot noir is something of a speciality here, with wines like Bara's Millésime, Comtesse Marie de France and Spécial Club.

Among the *récoltant-manipulants* there are no shortage of mavericks like Yannick **Doyard**, whose stylish, characterful wines have won a loyal following. Within his production of just over 50,000 bottles, you can find an old-style *oeil de perdrix* rosé and a special *cuvée* – *La Libertine* – with 60g/l of sugar, enough to satisfy even the most sweet-toothed Russian from the nineteenth century.

Also with vines in Bouzy, but mainly in Ambonnay and Verzenay, is Francis Egly, whose **Egly-Ouriet** champagnes are among the most prized in the whole of the Montagne de Reims. These include a pure pinot meunier called *Les Vignes de Vrigny* and *Les Crayères Vieilles Vignes*, a fabled Blanc de Noirs. With naturally low yields, just 12 hectares and a voracious fan club, new

TOP The family of Henri Goutorbe have accumulated 20 hectares of vineyards in Aÿ and its neighbouring villages since being set up during the First World War.

ABOVE Pierre Larmandier, the winemaker at Larmandier-Bernier, favours a biodynamic approach to champagne. His family owns 15 hectares of vineyards.

LEFT The big Houses may be the outward face of champagne in the market, but they rely on the growers who own 90% of the vineyards.

releases sell out fast. Meanwhile the **Gimonnet** family from Cuis in the Côte des Blancs boast 28 hectares and a history as growers stretching back to the mid-eighteenth century. They finally got round to selling the wine under the name Pierre Gimonnet in 1935. With vines now averaging over 40 years in age, the yields are slightly lower and the fruit that bit riper, meaning Didier and Olivier Gimonnet don't have to chaptalise their wines, unlike most producers in Champagne. Like Bollinger they keep some of their reserve wines in bottle.

In Bollinger's home village of Aÿ, the family of **Henri Goutorbe** were best known for their nursery, set up during the First World War to help replant the vineyards after phylloxera. It was a thriving business by all accounts and allowed the family to accumulate just over 20 hectares in Aÿ and neighbouring villages. With their sumptuous pinot noir fruit, the Goutorbes make a classy *Cuvée Tradition NV* and *Cuvée Prestige*, and a spectacular *Spécial Club Grand Cru*. All the wines are aged for at least three years on the lees.

At **Larmandier-Bernier**, winemaker Pierre Larmandier has been treading a biodynamic path since 2000 with much of the wine fermented in oak with wild yeast. The family own 15 hectares of the Côtes des Blancs in villages like Oger, Avize and Cramant, and have built up a glowing reputation for their crisp, mineral, low-*dosage* wines with chardonnay in the lead, or solo, role.

To the north, in the village of Gueus near Reims, the 2.2 hectares of pinot meunier inherited by **Jérôme Prévost** in 1987 would hardly seem the basis to go it alone as a *récoltant-manipulant*. But that's precisely what he did with the encouragement of Anselme Selosse some 10 years later. Today his intense, spicy, barrel-fermented wines have developed a serious cult following.

Selosse, whose wines are labelled **Jacques Selosse**, inherited his family's low-cropped vineyards in Avize, Cramant and Oger, to which he added small plots in Aÿ, Ambonnay and Mareuil. His wines are fermented in second-hand casks from some of the top estates in Burgundy and have an uncompromisingly earthy style that divides opinion. Some say they are overblown and oxidised, others love them with a passion. Either way they feel like a riposte to the big names out there with their consistent house styles and lifestyle marketing campaigns.

A few years after Selosse, **Erick De Sousa** took the plunge to become a **récoltant-manipulant** in 1986 with nine hectares of grand cru vineyards in Avize, Oger, Le Mesnil-sur-Oger, Chouilly and Grauves. The vines are farmed biodynamically, and tractors have given way to horses. Like a number of leading growers, he makes his top *cuvée des Caudalies*, in a *solera* system whereby the casks are refreshed with a new vintage each year to add a nutty, oaked character to the wines.

Finally to **Vilmart**, a grower champagne from the village of Rilly-la-Montagne in the Montagne de Reims which has been around since 1890, though its fame is much more recent. René Champs and his son Laurent have been a double act since 1989, when they created their complex, rich, invigorating *Coeur de Cuvée* that is four-fifths chardonnay. Though not quite in the same league, their 'basic' pinot noir-led Grande Réserve is pretty impressive too.

ABOVE *Coeur de Cuvée*, a champagne produced by Vilmart, ages in a cellar. It was first created by René and Laurent Champs in 1989.

BOTTOM LEFT Champagnes made by the grower Jacques Selosse are known for dividing opinion. They are fermented in second-hand casks from some of the top estates in Burgundy.

BELOW The spent lees in a bottle of Erick de Sousa's champagne. This grower producer began in 1986 and produces his *cuvée de caudalies* in a sherry-style *solera* system.

PART 4

SPARKLING WINES OF THE WORLD

IT HAS BEEN CHAMPAGNE'S GENIUS TO RISE ABOVE THE SEA OF MERE "SPARKLING WINE" AND PRESENT ITSELF AS SOMETHING UNIQUE – OFTEN COPIED BUT NEVER EQUALLED. OF COURSE, THE PRICE AND PRESTIGE OF ITS WINES HAVE ONLY ENCOURAGED OTHERS TO TRY USING THE SAME METHODS AND GRAPES. WHEN TASTED BLIND, SOME OF THESE CHAMPAGNE LOOKALIKES CAN BE VIRTUALLY INDISTINGUISHABLE FROM THE REAL THING, WHILE OTHERS ARE HAPPY TO BE JUST FROTHY, FRIVOLOUS AND FUN.

OPPOSITE Vineyards growing grapes for Cava in the Penedes region of Catalonia, north-east Spain. Cava, like Prosecco, has enjoyed dramatic worldwide growth in popularity in the early part of the 21st century.

PROSECCO

AT THE START OF THE THIRD MILLENNIUM FEW PEOPLE OUTSIDE OF ITALY AND GERMANY HAD HEARD OF PROSECCO WHICH SUDDENLY EXPLODED IN BRITAIN. DUBBED 'RECESSION CHAMPAGNE' DURING THE FINANCIAL CRASH OF 2008, ITS APPEAL HAS PROVED TO BE MUCH MORE ENDURING.

"When you are cutting your workforce and seeing your profits slide, the last thing you want to be seen doing is throwing champagne at some classy event," said Colin Tweedie, the head of Arts & Business, on the eve of its annual awards party in 2011. "It'll be the pop of a prosecco cork at this year's awards," he added. "No champagne I'm afraid."

Being inappropriate in times of an economic downturn is one of the downsides for champagne, with its glamourous and not exactly humble image. And yet it barely begins to explain the meteoric rise of prosecco whose global sales overtook champagne in around 2014. By the time of the 2018 vintage, the wine's total production was estimated to be around 600 million bottles give or take the odd bottle. Clearly the sparkler from the Veneto in north-east Italy is far more than just a cheap alternative to champagne when times are tough.

Like almost all sparkling wines, prosecco was inspired by champagne in the late nineteenth century when Antonio Carpenè treated his local white wine to some bottle fermentation. He was a professor of chemistry and in 1876 founded Italy's first school of oenology in the town of Conegliano, north of Venice. Some 20 years later, in north-west Italy a wine-maker called Federico Martinotti patented a new, far simpler way of making sparkling wine.

Martinotti thought that instead of fiddling around with a prolonged secondary fermentation in bottles, which then have to be riddled, disgorged and topped up as in Champagne, why not do the whole process in a sealed tank? The tank would be injected with yeast and kept under pressure to preserve the CO_2 in the wine. Tank fermentation, also known as the Charmat method or *Metodo Martinotti*, came to define Italian sparkling wine be it Asti Spumante or prosecco.

The 'P' word first appeared on a label when Antonio Carpenè's son, Etile, began to market a '*Prosecco Amabile dei Colli di*

FAR LEFT Antonio Carpenè, the founding father of Prosecco, whose pioneering efforts were made in champagne's image. Tank-fermented Prosecco came later.

LEFT A bunch of glera, which anyone can grow outside the land of Prosecco in north-east Italy and produce sparkling wine. The only rule is that they mustn't use the P-word.

OPPOSITE The wine's heartland, classified as Prosecco Superiore DOCG, lies in the conical hills north of Treviso.

Conegliano' in 1924. And yet for the next 50 years it was a slow burn for this local wine which hung out in bars from Verona to Venice and was drunk as a simple *brindisi*, or toast. Few if anyone in Champagne had ever heard of prosecco.

The first foreigners to embrace the wine were the Germans, who discovered it on holiday and brought the taste back home where it began to rival sales of home-grown *Sekt*. While the Brits needed a special occasion to crack open a bottle of sparkling wine, the Germans would be popping corks at any excuse so long as it was cheap. This was to lead to a big bust-up in the land of prosecco.

The original wine was named Prosecco DOC and came from the conical hills around Conegliano and Valdobiadenne, just north of Treviso, while the fizz produced on the Venetian plain, with fewer regulations was known as Prosecco IGT. These semantics mattered greatly to the producers up in the hills who were appalled at the level of abuse going on. There seemed little respect for the generous yields allowed under the IGT rules and what was exported in bulk was being mixed with God knows what to hit prices as low as €1.50 a bottle in German supermarkets.

The final straw was when an Austrian entrepreneur launched a canned version called Rich Prosecco in 2006, and hired Paris Hilton to promote it in the nude sprayed with gold paint in a stunt ripped from James Bond in the film *Goldfinger*. When she appeared on *Late Show with David Letterman* in the US, Ms Hilton explained that prosecco was Italian champagne. "Italian champagne? In a can? Champagne in a can!?" spluttered Letterman. "It's sexy," came the reply. "It looks great when you're holding it." Whether viewers were convinced seems unlikely.

"Basta!" (enough!) cried the Italians, who were suddenly galvanized into action. Prosecco DOC was extended from Trieste to Verona ,while the original area was upgraded to Prosecco Superiore DOCG. Yields were reduced, bulk exports were banned and crucially the Prosecco grape was rechristened Glera – presumably the ugliest synonym the producers could find. A small village was discovered near Trieste called Prosecco which somehow meant the whole area could be protected like Champagne. Anyone wishing to produce it outside the region was invited to call it Glera, or face the full might of Italian law. So far, but for the odd bottle of Brazilian or Australian prosecco sold locally, the Italians have been successful.

Having protected its borders, prosecco has surged in the USA and the UK – its biggest market – where it is now worth more than champagne and Spanish cava combined. Being tank-fermented and made from a different grape, the beauty of prosecco is that it is not trying to be champagne. It is frothy and frivolous and every day. In the words of Massimo Tuzzi, general manager of the big producer, Zonin: "If prosecco were a dress code it would be 'smart casual', as opposed to 'black tie' for champagne." Being softer, with a degree

BELOW Secondary fermentation takes just 30 days in pressurised stainless steel tanks.

less alcohol, it is a touch more forgiving the morning after. Also its relative sweetness being mainly Extra-Dry as opposed to *Brut* like virtually all champagne suggests our tastes may not be quite as bone dry as all that.

Meanwhile more and more vineyards are being turned over to prosecco production in the Veneto. Plantings on the plain grew by 3,000 hectares to 23,000 between 2015 and 2018 to produce 493 million bottles of Prosecco DOC, while the vineyards in the hills have effectively reached their limit of 5,000 hectares to produce around 100 million bottles of *Prosecco Superiore* DOCG. Some are already mentioning the possibility of a billion-bottle production, which may or may not include pink prosecco. As of 2018, the possibility of allowing a rosé version was still being debated.

When the UK's love affair with the Italian sparkler was at fever pitch in 2015, there was the terrifying prospect of a prosecco drought following a washout harvest the previous September. Middle England's worst nightmare was narrowly averted as bottles were released from the 2015 harvest just in time for Christmas. Production and demand continued to surge since then, until the Italian farming association, Coldiretti, announced that prosecco exports to the UK were down 7% in the first half of 2018.

The thought that Britain may have hit "peak prosecco" was sobering news for the Italians as sales in their biggest market had been on a steep upward trajectory for ten years. Coldiretti blamed

"the effects of Brexit" and "nationalistic fake news designed to discredit the Italian drink." This last point, an apparent reference to claims by a UK dentist that consumers who overindulged risked developing tooth decay which the press dubbed "a prosecco smile". But Brexit or not, the Italians clearly need to find some new drinkers beyond the Brits, Americans and Germans, who have been swallowing three-quarters of all prosecco exports.

BELOW LEFT Zonin, Italy's largest privately-owned wine business, is determined to build a strong brand that stands out from the sea of generic prosecco.

BELOW Paris Hilton with her infamous canned version in 2006. "It's sexy," she declared. "It looks great when you're holding it."

CAVA AND OTHER SPARKLING WINES

BEFORE PROSECCO BURST ONTO THE SCENE, CAVA WAS THE PRINCIPLE ALTERNATIVE FIZZ FOR THOSE ON A BUDGET. LIKE OTHER BOTTLE-FERMENTED WINES IT WAS MADE JUST LIKE CHAMPAGNE, ALBEIT FROM DIFFERENT GRAPES. TODAY VIRTUALLY EVERY WINE-PRODUCING NATION, INCLUDING INDIA, MAKES A SPARKLING WINE.

While the Italians were inventing sparkling prosecco, Josep Raventos returned from his European travels to create a Spanish sparkling wine to rival champagne at his family's winery of Codorníu in Penedès in 1872. This was the first of what became cava – the Spanish word for cellar, yet for some time it advertised itself as "Champagne Codorníu". Other producers soon joined in, selling their brands of Spanish champagne.

For much of the twentieth century, champagne producers considered it a brazen attempt to surf on the back of their fame and fortune, while the Spanish and others making sparkling wine argued that the "C" word had become pretty well generic. As we know, it was a battle the French eventually won, even succeeding in banning the term "*méthode champenoise*" within the EU in 1994 because no-one could agree a definition. Cava has been known as such since the 1970s, since when it is fair to say it has never really been associated with luxury fizz. For something made in champagne's image, it now finds itself in the ignominious position of competing toe to toe with tank-fermented prosecco. Indeed,

BELOW Bush-trained vines in the dry heat of Penedès.

despite the added costs of bottle fermentation for a minimum of nine months on the lees, cava is often discounted below the price of the Italian upstart.

Cava is traditionally produced from three local white grapes, with xarello said to provide the structure, parellada adding a certain creamy texture and macabeo giving freshness and acidity. That said, these are fairly neutral varieties, especially when picked early. Since 1959, the wine has had its own *Denominacion de Origin* (DO), or appellation, which now allows chardonnay in the blend, while the black grapes for pink *cava rosado* include pinot noir, garnacha and cabernet sauvignon.

In theory, the area of production is huge and covers eight regions from Rioja in the north-east to Extremadura in the west. In practice, cava is very much a Catalan wine, with around 95% coming from the Penedès region, just down the coast from Barcelona. The epicentre is the town of Sant Sadurní d'Anoia in the Alt Penedès which is home to the mighty Codorníu and Freixenet. A price war between these two brands, a surfeit of own-label cava in the supermarkets, and a somewhat coarse, yeasty character in some of the cheap stuff, conspired to drive down the wine's image.

Of the 250 million bottles of cava sold worldwide in 2017, only about 12% were of top quality, according to the cava regulatory council. The highest quality cava receives a Reserva or Gran Reserva label, which means it is matured for at least 24 months. There are plenty of quality-orientated producers, but they often struggle to stand out from the mass of cheap, commoditized cava. This has led to various breakaway movements like Corpinnat whose members come from a specified area of Penedès, grow their vines organically and age their wines for at least 18 months. As Xavier Gramona, one of the producers involved, told *The Guardian* in 2018: "We don't want to abandon the DO, but we need to add value so that the

ABOVE Bottles of Cordoníu waiting to be riddled by hand. In reality the process is all done mechanically by industrial *gyropalettes* well out of sight of any tourists.

LEFT A Cava-powered vehicle promoting Codorníu's great rival.

5,000 farmers who work in the sector can survive. In Champagne, a farmer with five hectares drives a Mercedes. Here, he can hardly make ends meet."

But the tide may be turning for cava whose quality has slowly improved in recent decades. Being grown in a relatively warm climate compared to most sparkling wine, there is less need for added sugar to balance the wine, and less need for pesticides in the vineyards. Stylistically cava tends to be bone dry without the hint of richness you can find in champagne, but the Spanish believe that makes it a good match for food. In London, this is being put to the test by a growing number of cava bars.

Back in France, sparkling wine extends far beyond champagne with bottle-fermented alternatives typically called crémant, as in Crémant de Loire, Crémant d'Alsace and Crémant de Limoux from the foothills of the Pyrenees. The latter was known as Blanquette de Limoux or originally Vin de Blanquette and claims to be the oldest sparkling wine in the world. It was a sweet, cloudy wine produced by the monks of the *Abbaye de Saint-Hilaire* that may have had bubbles when it first appeared in 1531. It is now clear and dry, but it is still made from the local mauzac grape.

Moving to Germany, a vast ocean of sparkling *Sekt* is produced, the vast majority tank-fermented from all manner of grapes unless called *Deutscher Sekt*, in which case the grapes have to be German. When made from Riesling, "the wines tend to be fresh, slightly floral, with plenty of apple and lime fruit flavours, and depending on the amount of time the fizz spends in contact with its lees, a touch of breadiness too," claims the drinks writer and master of wine, Patrick Schmitt. At the other end of the scale is cheap

FAR LEFT The Abbaye de Saint-Hilaire, the alleged birthplace of sparkling wine, 700 kilometres from Champagne.

LEFT Italy's top-selling brand of bottle-fermented sparkling wine comes from the mountainous vineyards of Trentino.

BELOW The town of Weinstadt, or "wine city" in the south-west German state of Baden-Wüttemberg, is surrounded by vineyards.

German *Schaumwein*, literally "foam wine", made from injecting CO2 as though via a soda stream and best avoided.

The Italians offer a number of bottle-fermented sparklers alongside prosecco and Asti spumante, of which the most famous is Franciacorta. This small appellation of 2,200 hectares lies between the northern city of Padua and the Lago d'Iseo. There have been local vineyards since Roman times, but the wine was still – until Franco Ziliani, winemaker at Berlucchi, created what was originally called Pinot di Franciacorta in 1961. By 2014 production was more than 16 million bottles with most being consumed in Lombardy, especially Milan. The wine has to be aged for a minimum of 18 months on the lees, rising to 60 months for the *Riserva*, and the grapes must be at least half pinot noir and chardonnay, and no more than half pinot blanc. Today it is rivalled by Trentodoc, a champagne look-alike from the foothills of the Dolomites, whose biggest brand is Ferrari. It's a nice name to have, but actually predates Enzo Ferrari and his four-wheeled version by 27 years.

The trouble with being a champagne look-alike is that it is hard to shake off the idea that you are a tribute band to "the real thing" back in France. Of course, this was no issue for the big champagne houses and their satellite operations that began with Moët & Chandon's Bodegas Chandon in Argentina, followed by Domaine Chandon in California in the 1970s. While there was always a risk that some Moët drinkers might be lost to these New World brand extensions, there was plenty of scope to recruit an army of new consumers. That it worked out was testament to the power of champagne, and before long other producers like Mumm, Taittinger and Roederer were heading to the Sunshine State to set up their own outposts.

When some pesky wine critics put Mumm champagne to the test in a blind tasting with its cheaper Cuvée Napa alternative and concluded the Californian version was better, the French

were unimpressed. "Personally," sniffed one of the leading *champenoise*, "I wouldn't compare blondes with brunettes." In 1986, Moët & Chandon took over an old dairy farm in Australia's Yarra valley called Green Point, though this time their venture was not copied by other champagne houses. The Australians have a vibrant sparkling wine industry of their own, particularly in Tasmania. In New Zealand there are now more than 100 producers of bottle-fermented fizz, particularly in Marlborough whose sauvignon vineyards were originally planted with that in mind. Today most New Zealand sparkling wine is from the classic trio of champagne grapes.

ABOVE Moët & Chandon was the first Champagne house to open a satellite operation in the Napa Valley in 1973.

LEFT The Yarra Valley, near Melbourne, has been home to Domaine Chandon – Moët & Chandon's Australian satellite – since 1986.

FOLLOWING PAGES Based in the Catalan town of Sant Sadurní d'Anoia – the epicentre of Cava production, Freixenet claims to be the world's largest producer of bottle-fermented fizz.

ENGLISH FIZZ

THE STORY OF CHAMPAGNE'S ORIGINS AS AN ANGLO-FRENCH CO-PRODUCTION (SEE PP30–31) WITH THE FRENCH PROVIDING THE BASE WINE AND THE ENGLISH THE STRONG GLASS AND A BIT OF SUGAR HAS, TO SOME EXTENT, COME FULL CIRCLE.

In late 2015, news broke that Taittinger was to become the first champagne house to make English sparkling wine, having bought a former Kent apple orchard in partnership with its UK agent, Hatch Mansfield. Forty hectares have been planted with chardonnay, pinot noir and pinot meunier to eventually produce 300,000 bottles of fizz.

The story had been a hardy perennial of the UK press – the sight of Frenchmen prospecting for vineyards across the Channel driven there by fears of global warming in Champagne. The fact that they returned empty-handed was a detail glossed over in excited reports in the *Daily Mail*, until Taittinger's news made it a reality. The first grapes were picked in 2018 and the first release of the wine, to be known as Domaine Evremond, is due in 2023. Yet Taittinger has been pipped at the post by Vranken-Pommery, thanks to a joint-venture with the Hampshire sparkling wine producer Hattingley Valley. Its Louis Pommery English sparkler is already on sale, and the French group has also planted its own 40-hectare vineyard in Hampshire.

Clovis Taittinger explained his firm's motives, saying: "We're doing it in a great spirit of friendship and because we believe we can produce a great sparkling wine in a great country. It's a way of saying, 'we love you, and want to do something fun for you.'" His father, Pierre-Emmanuel, gave a wonderfully Gallic reply when asked if English sparkling wine would ever rival champagne. "When things are good we don't talk about nationality. Mozart is Mozart. Alec Guinness is Alec Guinness. Brigitte Bardot is Brigitte Bardot," he said.

Producers of English fizz, whose production was around four million bottles in 2017, see things differently. They love nothing better than submitting to blind tastings and beating the French at their own game. It all started in the late 1980s at Nyetimber in West Sussex, where Sandy and Stuart Moss from Chicago ignored advice to grow apples and instead planted the three classic champagne grapes to make sparkling wine. Ten years later Nyetimber Classic Cuvée 1993 won the IWSR trophy for the world's best sparkling wine including champagne. "That's when people really sat up and took notice," says Julia Trustram-Eve, marketing director at WineGB.

"Competitions with the ability to pitch against what's recognized as the best of the best when it comes to sparkling wine, are absolutely vital," Julia continues, adding that winning such events is, "definitely proving to the outside world that English sparkling wines are right up there." But getting to this point has been quite some journey, considering the Romans were the first to plant vines in England, and that there were as many as 42 vineyards recorded in the Doomsday Book of 1085. After the "Medieval warm period", things turned decidedly chilly and the northern fringes of planet wine began to retreat back to France while imported wine became cheaper and more available.

By the 1950s, English wine had become an eccentric hobby, and in some cases a joke. Using Germanic hybrid varieties bred for a cold climate, it was a way to prove that you could make fermented grape juice, though whether you should was sometimes less obvious.

BELOW In 2015, Pierre-Emmanuel Taittinger (on the right) was delighted to announce a joint venture with his English importer Hatch Mansfield, to become the first Champagne House to invest in English vineyards in 2015.

It tended to be still wine, whereas the proximity of Champagne clearly suggested it would be worth trying sparkling wine. The need for a relatively neutral, acidic base wine was something a reasonable summer in southern England could usually achieve. Another clue lay in the ground because the same band of chalk that breaks through the surface of the Côte des Blancs in Champagne reappears in the white cliffs of Dover and on the South Downs.

If you select the right slope on the right soil, which is as sun-drenched and sheltered as possible, and match it with the most suitable clones of chardonnay, pinot noir and pinot meunier, you are

FAR LEFT Founded in 2008, Hampshire's Hattingley Valley released its first wine five years later..

LEFT Nyetimber's victory in the IWSR awards as the "world's best sparkling wine" in 1993, was a defining moment for English fizz.

BELOW Grapes being picked in a vineyard in West Chiltington, near Pulborough in Sussex, destined for Nyetimber.

FOLLOWING PAGES Glowing candles at Ridgeview in Sussex in April 2017 to try and protect the emerging buds from a late spring frost

in with a chance of producing a good sparkling wine. And it is not just Nyetimber, as a growing number of award-winning producers, such as Ridgeview, Camel Valley, Chapel Down, Hush Heath and Coates & Sealey among others, have shown.

Global warming may be one factor, though to suggest that Tunbridge Wells is the new Épernay, as one English producer has claimed, is stretching things. As many point out, the South Coast may be close as the crow flies, but the climate is temperate and maritime compared to the more continental weather system in Champagne. Similarly, while some producers wax lyrical about the magical mix of chalk and chardonnay in their vineyards, those of Nyetimber's for example are mainly sand and clay.

There are now more than 500 commercial vineyards planted in the UK from Cornwall to Northumberland with the most northerly sparkling wine coming from Leventhorpe. within the city boundary of Leeds. As of 2017, there were 2,500 hectares of vines, of which three-quarters were in Sussex, Kent and Hampshire, but that figure could grow exponentially according to a report in 2018 by the University of East Anglia (UEA). "We wanted to identify the best places to plant vineyards and improve the sector's resilience to the UK's often fickle weather," explained Professor Steve Dorling of the UEA's School of Environmental Sciences. England and Wales were mapped out in 50m2 plots and nearly 35,000 hectares of potential "prime viticultural land" were identified. Essex and Suffolk were

LEFT English vineyards could spread exponentially and may one day rival the 34,500 hectares planted in Champagne.

BELOW The same strata of chalk that breaks through the topsoil in the Côte des Blancs in Champagne, resurfaces across the English Channel in the White Cliffs of Dover.

considered to be particularly promising.

This neatly matches the 34,500 hectares planted in Champagne, though English production per hectare tends to be around half the French average, except in years like 2018 which was declared a fantastic vintage in terms of yield and quality. Yet only six years earlier the cold wet summer had meant producers like Nyetimber decided not to pick any grapes at all. As Dr Alistair Nesbitt, the lead author of the UEA report concluded: "Entering into viticulture and wine production isn't for the faint hearted – the investment required is high and the risks are significant."

That said, there definitely is a buzz around English wine right now and a growing self-confidence. "We are experiencing a phenomenal rate of growth," says Julia Trustram-Eve, pointing to current plantings of more than one million vines a year. Extrapolating the growth and using the experience of Oregon's wine industry as a model, WineGB predict English wine could be worth £1 billion by 2040, from sales of 40 million bottles. Of that, a good two-thirds will be sparkling wine, which is bound to impact champagne's biggest export market by volume as of 2017. No doubt other champagne houses will follow Taittinger and Pommery and cross the Channel armed with their cheque books, what with an acre of potential land costing less than a tenth of what you would pay in Champagne. Meanwhile farmers along the South Coast blessed with the right land can start to dream of replanting that field of turnips and maybe one day producing a nectar to rival Krug or Dom Pérignon.

For now English sparkling wine appears to be enjoying something of a honeymoon period, and as it evolves there will be plenty of challenges ahead and not just from the weather gods. The next stage will see the wines begin to assume their own identity free from champagne's shadow, but it will be a slow process with the latter enjoying a 300-year head-start. Despite using the same mix of grapes from an often similar chalky *terroir* and using the same production methods, there are subtle differences. Nyetimber's winemaker Cherie

Spriggs, who was crowned sparkling winemaker of the year in the 2018 IWC awards, points to the slightly longer growing time in England. In Sussex it averages around 105 days between bud burst and harvest, compared to 95 in Champagne. There is also the effect of having slightly longer daylight hours in summer.

"I find a characteristic of English sparkling wine is its purity, driven by acidity and freshness, whereas I feel in Champagne there is a slightly stronger emphasis on autolysis," says Julia, referring to those toasty, brioche notes that come from long bottle ageing. Yet when English and French sparklers are pitched together in blind tastings it can be very hard to tell them apart. Such tastings are bound to continue and, before long, someone is sure to test Taittinger against its English satellite. Will it win? Who knows?

ABOVE Ridgeview's wines carry a dedication to Christopher Merret, who first documented the process of producing a traditional method sparkling wine in England in 1662.

BELOW In 2018 Kent-based Chapel Down announced plans to create England's largest vineyard capable of producing up to a million bottles of sparkling wine.

PART 5

CULTURE AND TRADITIONS

BY THE START OF THE TWENTIETH CENTURY, NOTHING ANNOUNCED YOU HAD 'ARRIVED' QUITE LIKE THE POP OF A CHAMPAGNE CORK. WRITERS, ARTISTS AND FILM DIRECTORS FOUND THE SYMBOLISM IRRESISTIBLE, WHETHER TO PORTRAY WEALTH, STATUS, DECADENCE OR VICE. CHAMPAGNE HAS LONG BEEN FAR MORE THAN JUST A DRINK.

OPPOSITE That champagne and celebration are joined at the hip is confirmed with every glass clinked together.

"LIE BACK AND THINK OF FRANCE"

THE CHAMPAGNE HOUSE OF E. DEBRAY HAS LONG DISAPPEARED, BUT ITS NAME LIVES ON IN A GLORIOUSLY EFFERVESCENT POSTER BY THE ARTIST PIERRE BONNARD THAT WAS PASTED ALL OVER PARIS IN THE SPRING OF 1891. THE TITLE, IN BOLD, SWIRLING CAPITALS DECLARES IT IS "FRANCE-CHAMPAGNE".

The poster depicts a curvy young woman, open-mouthed and eyes closed in ecstasy, clutching a glass overflowing with a frothing tide of fizz. Almost toppling out of her dress, if not the poster itself, she is the very essence of French *joie de vivre*.

The fame of champagne and its global success is clearly a source of pride to the French. It is the country's great sparkling ambassador around the world and offers a flattering reflection of the national psyche, brimming with wit and charm. For Voltaire: "The effervescence of this fresh wine reveals the true brilliance of the French people," while Bonnard's contemporary, Adolphe Brisson, claimed: "It is made in our image: it sparkles like our intellect." A little bombastic perhaps, even by French standards, but one imagines most Frenchmen would be suitably chuffed if you came to the same conclusion.

Of course, champagne does not reflect the whole of French society, only a part of it. In *When Champagne Became French*, Kolleen Guy includes a print from the time of the French Revolution called 'L'Accord fraternel' in which members of the Three Estates toast each other. The common man in his tricorn hat raises a glass of simple *vin rouge*. The clergyman does the same with some Burgundy, while a soldier, representing the aristocracy, lifts a dainty flute of champagne. This demonstrates plenty of *fraternité* and *liberté*, but not quite so much *égalité*. The truth is, champagne has always enjoyed an elite image as something to aspire to.

It wasn't the only product sold with added snob appeal. In her book, Guy unearths a lovely gem from the *Edinburgh Review* of 1834, advertising 'Mr Cockle's Antibilious Pills' as recommended by "ten dukes, five marquises, seventeen earls, eight viscounts,

ABOVE An English magazine advert from the 1920s proudly proclaiming Bollinger's royal warrant for its Special Cuvée.

FAR LEFT The rosy-cheeked Madame de Pompadour, Louis XV's mistress, was a tremendous fan of champagne and claimed it was the only wine that left a woman feeling more beautiful.

LEFT From an early affiliation with hot-air balloons, champagne progressed to powered flight. This poster promoted the first true aviation meeting on the plains north of Reims in 2009.

sixteen lords …" and, presumably a partridge in a pear tree. Champagne brands battled to win those precious 'by appointment' contracts to European courts from Queen Victoria to the Russian Czars. At the same time the brand-owners were marrying off their daughters to the *ancien régime* and acquiring titles along the way. Concerns that the merchants might be a little *nouveau riche* were brushed aside for practical reasons. It takes deep pockets to keep the roof on the old family château.

The expense of delivering bubbles in a bottle that didn't explode came down thanks to improved technology in the cellar just as incomes rose among the new middle classes. When the two met in the middle, in the latter half of the nineteenth century, champagne took off. There was no better way to announce you had 'arrived' than that explosive pop of a champagne cork. This was a universal truth from Bristol to Baltimore, but there was something very French about the way the drink was sold. Brands may have been by appointment to royalty and have fancy coats of arms on their labels, but the market was the burgeoning bourgeoisie. French tastes in fashion, above all in food and drink, were what middle-class consumers deferred to all over the world.

While the word *champagne* is masculine in French, it was the country's women who were recruited to advertise the brands, employing all their sex appeal. Today you are not allowed to imply any alcoholic drink might boost your prowess in the bedroom, least of all in France with its draconian *Loi Evin*, but rules were more relaxed in the past. Alongside heroic figures like Jean of Arc and Marianne, the symbol of the French Republic, were an endless cast of *femmes fatales*. They were sophisticated, worldly wise and full of seductive charm. For men, those wicked bubbles might help to loosen a bodice or two, while for women, champagne was the only wine that left you feeling more beautiful, according to Louis XV's mistress, Madame de Pompadour.

Champagne almost became too universal, and it took the combined muscle of the CIVC, and its predecessors, along with the French state, to fully protect its name from all those seeking to use it elsewhere in France and beyond. With total sales now edging towards €5 billion a year, it is the country's top food and drink export, accounting for one-third of all French wine shipments by value. As protected *appellations* go, its success is second only to Scotch whisky. Other French wines have struggled due to domestic consumption halving in the space of a generation and the advent of competition from the New World, while champagne goes from strength to strength.

Champagne has seeped into every moment of celebration from the most intimate to the most public, from a quiet, family christening to the baptism of a towering new liner. While the location might be some shipyard on the other side of the world, a little piece of France will come swinging through the air to burst against the hull as the ship slips into the water. The idea of launching such a vessel with a bottle of cava or Prosecco would be quite unthinkable.

With a good 150 years of practice, the drink has helped the French perfect the art of luxury goods marketing like no one else. And none more so than the mighty LVMH, or Louis Vuitton Moët Hennessy, whose champagne brands include Krug, Dom Pérignon and Veuve Clicquot. As the American wine economist, Mike Veseth, observed: "Champagne is famous, because it isn't really just wine. It is really fame (and luxury) itself."

TOP Ships from all four corners of the world are routinely baptised with champagne. The idea of using Prosecco would be almost unthinkable.

ABOVE Champagne has helped the French perfect the art of luxury goods marketing, and none more that the great power house of Louis Vuitton Moët Hennessy.

CHAMPAGNE IN ART AND LITERATURE

AN EARLY PASSAGE FROM *THE GREAT GATSBY* FINDS NARRATOR NICK CARRAWAY DRAWN TO HIS LONG ISLAND NEIGHBOUR. LATER IN SCOTT FITZGERALD'S GREAT AMERICAN NOVEL, THE FIZZ STILL FLOWS, BUT CARRAWAY DETECTS A SOUR NOTE HAS CREPT IN WHILE OBSERVING ONE OF GATSBY'S PARTIES FROM THE INSIDE.

Carraway first noted: "There was music from my neighbour's house through the summer nights. In his blue gardens men and girls came and went like moths among the whisperings and the champagne and the stars."

Later, however:

> *"There were the same people, or at least the same sort of people, the same profusion of champagne, the same many-colored, many-keyed commotion, but I felt an unpleasantness in the air, a pervading harshness that hadn't been there before."*

It was the 1920s, with the Jazz Age in full swing, even if America was theoretically dry due to Prohibition. What else but champagne could reflect the glamour and status of this dazzling socialite who was rumoured to have made his fortune as a bootlegger? The truth is, no other drink packs the same symbolic punch, and for novelists it has always been shorthand for opulence, decadence and excess. When Evelyn Waugh satirised Oxford's Bullingdon club in *Decline and Fall*, he called it the Bollinger club and filled it with "the upper classes braying for the sound of broken glasses".

Champagne has allure even for those selling it. In Arthur Miller's *Death of a Salesman*, Willy Loman's son Happy tries to impress a girl in a restaurant by telling her: "I sell champagne, and I'd like you to try my brand." Then, having asked the waiter to bring her a glass, he says she ought to be on the cover of a magazine, before adding: "You know what they say in France, don't you? Champagne is the drink of the complexion …" As the audience, we know it's all complete fantasy, as Happy's real job is assistant to the assistant buyer at the local store.

Oscar Wilde couldn't resist mentioning his favourite champagne, Perrier-Jouët, in *The Importance of Being Earnest*, and even had a case of it delivered to his cell after his conviction for 'the love that dare not speak its name'. And when ordering one last glass on his deathbed in 1900, he allegedly turned to his doctor, and sighed: "Alas, I am dying beyond my means."

The Russian playwright, Anton Chekhov, followed suit when he died four years later, as his wife recorded in a letter: "… he picked up

BELOW LEFT AND RIGHT   Working in Paris at the turn of the century, Czech artist Alphonse Mucha transformed the art of the poster. These classic lithographs for Moët are a great example.

the glass, turned to me, smiled his wonderful smile and said: 'It's been such a long time since I've had champagne.' He drank it all to the last drop, quietly lay on his left side and was soon silent forever."

Of countless other literary mentions, among the best is this pearl of wisdom from Graham Greene in *Travels with My Aunt*.

"Champagne, if you are seeking the truth, is better than a lie detector. It encourages a man to be expansive, even reckless, while lie detectors are only a challenge to tell lies successfully."

Earlier, Aunt Augusta explains the virtues of flying first class to Paris, because "you can guzzle all the free champagne and make up the difference in cost."

Perhaps there are fewer champagne references in art, but the time and place to look for them is *fin-de-siècle* Paris when Post-Impressionist painters like Pierre Bonnard were in town. It was winning a competition to produce an advertising poster entitled 'France Champagne' in 1889 that encouraged Bonnard to abandon a career in the law and become an artist. The famous lithograph was reproduced all over Paris and inspired many others. All manner of pre-Raphaelite beauties began to appear in prints to promote different brands of champagne.

The English artist Walter Crane painted an allegorical female figure to advertise the long-forgotten Champagne House of Hau & Co. She is entwined with vines in golden, autumnal colours, resting a jug on her shoulder and holding a champagne *coupe* in an outstretched hand. Meanwhile the Czech painter and decorative artist Alphonse Mucha worked for Hiedsieck and Moët & Chandon at the turn of the century. For the latter he depicted a brunette with a high-necked dress and ornate jewellery to capture the essence of Moët's dry Imperial. For the brand's White Star, Mucha chose a sensual blonde with bare shoulders in a pink dress.

Bonnard's lithograph also inspired his friend Henri de Toulouse-Lautrec to create equally vivid prints, famously in his series for the Moulin Rouge when it flung open its doors at the foot of Montmartre in 1889. While less directly connected with champagne, and with a personal penchant for absinthe in good artistic tradition, Toulouse-Lautrec's art came to symbolise the city at night. As a cabaret venue, the Moulin Rouge was an iconic institution during the period that offered a cocktail of risqué sophistication. Champagne soaked up this imagery of Parisian nightlife and beamed it back around the world. The drink both fuelled the Belle Époque and fed off its image.

The other great Parisian venue was the Folies-Bergère, which opened 20 years earlier, and this was the subject of Édouard Manet's last major work in 1882 and one of his finest. *A Bar at the Folies-Bergère* features a sad-eyed barmaid in front of a giant mirror that plays an optical trick with the viewer. She seems to be staring into space, until we realise from the mirror she is engaged with a shadowy figure in a top hat. In front of her are bottles of champagne on one side and a bowl of oranges on the other. The fruit signifies she is a prostitute.

TOP The champagne-loving Oscar Wilde had a thing about Perrier-Jouët. He even had a case delivered to his cell when he began his prison sentence in 1895.

ABOVE Like Oscar Wilde, only four years later, Anton Chekhov died with the taste of champagne on his lips.

LEFT The gleaming gold-topped bottles of champagne in the foreground and the vast chandelier in the mirror suggest opulent glamour in Édouard Manet's *A Bar at the Folies-Bergère*, but the barmaid's eyes say something else.

RIGHT The famous music hall song premiered in the Princess' Concert Hall in Leeds in the summer of 1866.

OPPOSITE Ariana Grande released "Pink Champagne" in a YouTube video for her 10 million Twitter fans in 2013.

CELLULOID CHAMPAGNE

THE POWER OF CHAMPAGNE TO CONVEY GLAMOUR, DECADENCE AND WEALTH HAS LONG BEEN A GIFT TO FILMMAKERS. THE WINE'S VIVACITY AND SPARKLE WERE SOMEHOW MADE FOR THE SILVER SCREEN, WHICH ALSO BENEFITS FROM THE EVOCATIVE POP OF THE CORK.

The camera can pull back to take in the champagne-swilling guests at a party, or zoom in to capture the bubbles dancing in a glass. As for sound, audiences had to imagine the pop in Alfred Hitchcock's silent movie *Champagne*, released in 1928 just before the advent of the 'talkies'. It opens and closes with a shot through the bottom of a giant champagne glass that the director had specially made. The film claimed to have "a light, frivolous, frothy character interspersed with touches of tense drama" giving its star, Betty Balfour, the chance to "display her wonderfully vivacious and appealing personality". The critics disagreed, and Hitch later admitted: "The film had no story to tell."

Much more successful was Greta Garbo's first full-length comedy *Ninotchka* in 1939, in which she plays a stern Russian official in Paris, where she is seduced by a French count with the help of champagne. Having only seen it used to launch battleships back home, she tells him: "From what I read I thought champagne was a strong drink. It's very delicate," and then, knocking back a glassful, adds: "Do people ever get drunk on this?" Needless to say, she is soon completely legless.

A year later, James Stewart, Cary Grant and Katharine Hepburn teamed up for the beguiling, screwball comedy *The Philadelphia Story*. On its re-release in 2015, the film critic Peter Bradshaw described how: "The fun and wit rise like champagne bubbles, but there is a deceptive strength in the writing and performances." In one scene, Stewart, playing a prickly journalist, is the most elegant drunk ever to appear on screen. He swerves into Grant's driveway by car one night and emerges clutching a bottle and a paper cup. "Cinderella's slipper," he declares. "It's called champagne. Champagne is a great leveller. It makes you my equal."

And then came *Casablanca*, the ultimate romantic drama in which champagne has a small walk-on part. "Henri wants us to finish this bottle, then three more," says Rick Blaine (Humphrey Bogart) to Ilsa Lund (Ingrid Bergman). "He says he'll water his garden with champagne before he lets the Germans drink any of it." The film came out in 1942, while the Nazis were busy importing as much as possible via their *weinführer* in Reims, Otto Klaebisch.

After the war, the warm embrace between champagne and the movies became more business-like. The studio moguls needed fizz, but they soon sussed the brand-owners would pay for the privilege, such was the glamour of Hollywood and the competition among the Champagne Houses. And on this score, no franchise could match 007. Ian Fleming liked Taittinger, and this was his hero's preferred sparkler in the books. But the brand's film career was cut short in 1963, when a glass was spiked with poison in *From Russia with Love*. Claude Taittinger allegedly refused to have any further involvement with the Broccoli clan. Dom Pérignon stepped in, prompting some of the worst lines in the series. "My dear girl, there are some things that just aren't done, such as drinking Dom Pérignon '53 above the temperature of 38 degrees Fahrenheit," says

an insufferably priggish, patronising Bond. "That's just as bad as listening to the Beatles without earmuffs!"

By the time *Live and Let Die* appeared in 1973, Bollinger had oiled its way in and has never looked back. Soon the cheesy *double-entendres* were coming thick and fast with Roger Moore in the title role. "Bollinger?" he says with a smirk to CIA agent Holly Goodhead in *Moonraker*. "If it's the '69, you were expecting me." This play on vintages became an easy way to separate the goodies from the baddies. In *A View to a Kill*, Bond, now played by Roger Moore, takes a sip of champagne and declares it to be Bollinger '75, which impresses detective Achille Aubergine (played by Jean Rougerie) no end. "I see you are a connoisseur." This is all it takes to convince the ridiculous-sounding Frenchman that Bond is who he says he is.

Looking back, it appears the series was rescued just in time before it disappeared into a black hole of self-parody. But such are the costs of production; brands are hired and fired on the set of James Bond. Heineken's 'blink and you'll miss it' appearance in *Skyfall* apparently covered nearly 30% of the film's £98 million production budget. Cynics may wonder if today's scriptwriters simply type in the word 'drink' whenever 007 needs to slake his thirst, and the slot is later auctioned to the highest bidder. If you ever catch Bond bedding down with a bottle of Buckfast you'll know why.

Back in the 1920s, novelists like the champagne-loving F. Scott Fitzgerald never mentioned any particular brand in their books. But in Baz Luhrmann's 2013 remake of *The Great Gatsby*, the production designer Catherine Martin decided it had to be Moët

& Chandon that flowed through pyramid fountains of glasses and poured from giant-sized bottles. Nothing speaks of wealth and excess quite like a Balthazar or Nebuchadnezzar of champagne. LVMH, the owners of the brand, were apparently delighted, though what the agreement was with Warner Bros. is a closely guarded secret.

One other film to mention is the 1992 American comedy *Wayne's World*. "I don't believe I've ever had French champagne before," says Cassandra (Tia Carrere). "Oh, actually all Champagne is French; it's named after the region. Otherwise it's sparkling white wine," replies Benjamin Oliver (Rob Lowe). The CIVC couldn't have put it better.

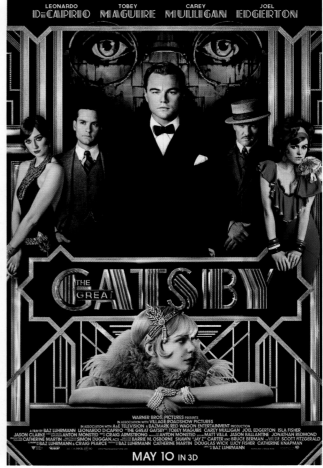

RIGHT Hitchcock's 1928 silent film *Champagne* lacked sparkle according to the critics. For the American entertainment magazine *Variety* it was: "an excuse for covering 7,000 feet of harmless celluloid with legs and close-ups."

OPPOSITE Bond has been known to drink other champagnes including Dom Perignon and Taitinger, but latterly he's stayed loyal to Bollinger

VISITING CHAMPAGNE

CHAMPAGNE HAS ALWAYS BEEN THE MOST ACCESSIBLE WINE REGION, TRAIPSED OVER BY MERCHANTS, PILGRIMS AND FOREIGN AGGRESSORS FROM ATTILA THE HUN TO THE NAZIS. TODAY'S VISITORS COME IN PEACE TO SOAK UP THE PASTORAL LANDSCAPE AND ABOVE ALL THE WINE, IN A REGION RECENTLY GRANTED UNESCO WORLD HERITAGE STATUS.

Emerging from the mouth of the Channel tunnel on the French side, it is a comfortable three-hour drive to the heart of Champagne, while if you fly to Paris, Charles de Gaulle, it is a 30-minute TGV rail journey to Reims (note: it is roughly pronounced '*raance*', with a soft 'n', and not '*reems*'). This is the commercial hub of the region and home to a bevy of important Champagne Houses from the oldest, Ruinart, to the grandees of Krug and Roederer, to the likes of Pommery and Taittinger among others. There are said to be a billion bottles, give or take, quietly undergoing a secondary fermentation in the maze of subterranean cellars beneath the streets. It makes you wonder – a slight tectonic shift and Reims would collapse through the earth's crust in a crescendo of exploding glass.

The city's Roman entrance to the north – the Porte de Mars – still stands, as does the Abbaye St Remi and the Jesuit college to the south, but the German artillery flattened just about everything else in between during the First Word War. Rebuilt with art deco flourishes in the 1920s and with a restored cathedral, Reims inevitably lacks

the history of other medieval towns in the region. On the plus side it has some of the best-preserved Gallo-Roman tunnels, especially at Taittinger. Also look out for the impressive bas-relief carvings in the cellars of Pommery, whose old family mansion has been transformed into Les Crayères, the swankiest boutique hotel in the whole of Champagne.

The unofficial 'capital of champagne' is Épernay, half an hour by train south of Reims, and almost one-eighth the size and prettier with its backdrop of vine-clad slopes. Here there is no escaping fizz, especially if you strut down the Avenue de Champagne where the HQs of the big Houses vie to outdo each other. The country château-style Pol Roger at No. 44 was dubbed "the most drinkable address in Europe" by its top fan – Sir Winston Churchill. Jean-Rémy Moët, not content with just one palace, built a replica across the street, known as *La Résidence Trianon*, for Napoleon and his entourage when they headed east. Between Moët & Chandon at No. 20 and Pol

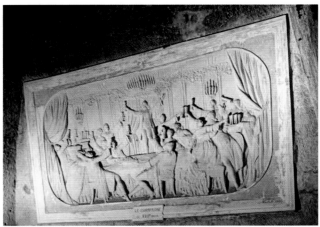

MIDDLE LEFT Patchwork vineyards within the *Parc naturel regional de la Montagne de Reims* (Reims Mountain Regional Natural Park), famed for its pinot noir.

BELOW The Porte de Mars in Reims, a Roman triumphal arch from the third century AD, was one of the few structures to survive the German artillery in the First World War.

BOTTOM LEFT The bas-relief carved into the chalk walls of Pommery's cellars in Reims, have greeted visitors since the 1870s, when Louise Pommery created a top tourist attraction with her Theatre of Champagne.

Roger, lie Mercier and Perrier-Jouët, all of which you can visit for a fairly pricey guided tour of around €20 with a glass of bubbly thrown in.

With some Houses you can just turn up, others you have to book, while a few are simply too grand to open their doors, but you probably need to do one such visit before venturing out into the villages. This is where the real joy of Champagne lies and if you stay in a gîte run by a grower producer – and many do B&B on the side – you will begin to feel much more like a native. In markets like the UK, dominated by perhaps a dozen big brands, the choice of champagne in Champagne is mind-blowing. But help is at hand if you go to: www.vigneron-independent-champagne.com, which narrows the field to 300 or so. Most will happily show you round, give you a little tasting and sell you some fizz, which is just how the Parisians buy their champagne. Their logo – a woodcut of a grower with a barrel on his back – is easy to spot.

You can avoid Reims and Épernay altogether and make an appointment to visit one of the other grand marques like Bollinger in Aÿ or Joseph Perrier in Châlons-en-Champagne, as well as local grower producers. Alternatively you can head south to arguably the prettiest part of the region and the rolling countryside of the Aube. The region's capital, connected with a direct train from Paris, is the half-timbered, almost Bavarian-like town of Troyes. You may not find the glitz and glamour of Épernay's Grands Marques, but possibly something more authentic.

Recommended reading: Philippe Boucheron's *Destination Champagne*

WORLD HERITAGE STATUS FOR CHAMPAGNE

In early July 2015, 'the vineyards, cellars and champagne houses' of the region were granted World Heritage status by UNESCO, the United Nations' cultural arm. It was one of 11 sites around the world, including the Botanic Gardens of Singapore and Iran's ancient city of Susa. For the Champenois it was a sweet victory and the culmination of a long campaign. UESCO's rules permit each country to submit only two candidates a year. Champagne had failed to make the grade on its last attempt two years earlier.

Apparently the UNESCO panel had been particularly impressed by the vineyards of Aÿ and Mareuil-sur-Aÿ and the chalk cellars dug into the St Niçaise hill in Reims during Gallo-Roman times. At the same time parts of Burgundy were also declared a World Heritage site, joining wine regions that include Portugal's Douro valley, Tokaj in Hungary and the Mosel valley in Germany.

For Champagne it was a vindication of how much has changed since the 1980s, when the vineyards were drenched with chemical sprays to kill off bugs and boost yields in a desperate bid to match demand. Since the Millennium a more sustainable approach is being adopted, though the pressure is intense in a region already at peak production. It won't be until 2020 that any wine from the 40 new villages will come on stream. In the meantime the price of supermarket champagne may have to become a little more sustainable too.

ABOVE Château Les Crayères, a swanky hotel and Michelin-starred restaurant standing next to Champagne Pommery in Reims and built by Pommerys in the early 1900s.

FOLLOWING PAGES There are no shortage of well-signed tourist trails through the region, linking the famous champagne villages.

A SPARKLING INVESTMENT

CHAMPAGNE IS FOR DRINKING, BUT SOME BOTTLES ARE SO RARE THEIR OWNERS DISPLAY THEM BEHIND GLASS LIKE PRECIOUS JEWELS, OR KEEP THEM HIDDEN IN A BONDED WAREHOUSE AND TRADE THEM FOR PROFIT.

In 2015 you could pop in to Aldi and buy a bottle of Veuve Monsigny NV champagne for £10.99. Produced by Philizot & Fils with "aromas of baked apples, brioche and stone fruits" according to Aldi, it was the country's favourite champagne, accounting for one in 12 bottles sold that year. Alternatively you could head for Hedonism Wines in London's Mayfair, where champagne prices reach the dizzy heights of £26,123.40 for a magnum of Krug 1937, signed by Rémi Krug himself.

This is to illustrate the extremes within the world of champagne, with the latter example very much at the collectible, investment end of the spectrum. Whether the Krug '37 will increase much further in value is debatable, but there is no doubt its worth must have soared since the vintage was first released, probably in the 1940s. If you want to make a killing on champagne, it all depends on when you buy and when you sell, though obviously you first need to pick the right bottles. Investing in Aldi's bargain bubbles would not yield much of a return.

Those who speculate in fine wine are one leg of a three-legged stool, the others being collectors and well-heeled consumers, though obviously in practice they might be one and the same. If prices rise so high that drinkers and/or collectors, are priced out, the stool is liable to collapse. Investors rely on others to diminish the supply by drinking these rarefied bottles and thereby boosting the value of what remains. Luckily for them it seems there are still plenty of extremely rich people out there with an appetite for fizz.

Probably most fancy champagnes sold by merchants like Hedonism will be drunk, perhaps on a Russian yacht. Investors prefer to buy at auction or from fine wine traders, and keep their stash in a temperature-controlled bonded warehouse. That way, they are kept safe and sound, and free from temptation. Stored under the stairs, it would be all too easy to crack open the bottles in a moment of reckless abandon among friends, though arguably that is precisely what champagne was invented for.

The names to look out for when it comes to 'investment-grade' champagne are as follows: Dom Pérignon, Krug, Louis Roederer Cristal, Taittinger Comtes de Champagne, Salon Cuvée 'S' Le Mesnil, Philipponnat, Clos des Goisses, plus the top wines of Ruinart, Bollinger and Pol Roger. Pricing relates to the prestige of the House and the scores of the leading critics for the particular release. But as in Bordeaux, producers will be furtively looking over their shoulders to see what their rivals are charging. The prices paid represent a form of ranking for the top Houses, and a reaffirmation of their status.

Production of these prestige *cuvées* tends to be very small. For example, Salon Mesnil release fewer than 3,000 cases a year, while for Cristal it is fewer than 25,000 cases. The sales are tracked on a weekly basis by Liv-ex, which operates like a mini-stock market or trading platform for such wines. While the top châteaux of Bordeaux dominate the trade, Liv-ex reports a growing interest in champagne with investors keen to diversify their portfolio.

Top champagnes appear to have been more stable, though you do need to have patience. "Signs of appreciation are visible amongst vintages earlier than and including the 2000," Liv-ex concluded in a report in late 2015. It gave Taittinger's 1996 vintage champagne as an example, recording how it was first traded at £630 a case in June 2003, and had reached £1,896 just 12 years later. Yet clearly prices can go the other way, as happened to Bordeaux's Grands Crus, which peaked in June 2011. They then crashed by a third, which is either "a burst bubble" or just a "market correction", depending on who is speaking.

"Of course the great advantage of wine, is that even if it is not worth as much as it was the year before it will probably taste better. So at least you get to drink your investment even if you can't cash it in," said Simon Berry, chairman of Berry Bros & Rudd, in a BBC Four documentary about the famous London wine merchant.

Consumption is clearly not an option for other alternative investments like gold, oil or carbon credits, but knowing that a particular wine has slumped in value might affect one's appreciation of it. What's that distinctive aroma lurking behind those notes of brioche and toasted almonds, if not the scent of sour grapes?

BELOW Amber nectar poured from a 200-year-old bottle of champagne in 2010, having been rescued by divers from a shipwreck in the Baltic Sea near the Finnish Aaland islands.

OPPOSITE Gleaming bottles of 'investment-grade champagne' – in this case, Louis Roederer Cristal.

AUCTIONS

Along with releases like the Krug Collection, dribbled out on to the secondary market, are really old, rare bottles that crop up at auction. Their value will be affected by the reliability of their provenance, and the condition they are in, although exceptions are made. In 2010, divers exploring a shipwreck off the Åland Islands, in the Baltic Sea, discovered a stash of champagne bottles dating from the 1820s. The labels had long disintegrated, but from the corks, three were identified with "absolute certainty" as Veuve Clicquot, whose then winemaker Francis Hautekeur was lucky enough to try some. He claimed it had, "a toasty, zesty nose with hints of coffee and a very agreeable taste, with accents of flowers and lime."

One bottle of this ancient Veuve Clicquot was sold at auction in New York in June 2011 for US$43,630 (£26,675/€30,400), a world-record price for champagne, just eclipsing the previous record for a 1959 Dom Pérignon Rosé in 2008.

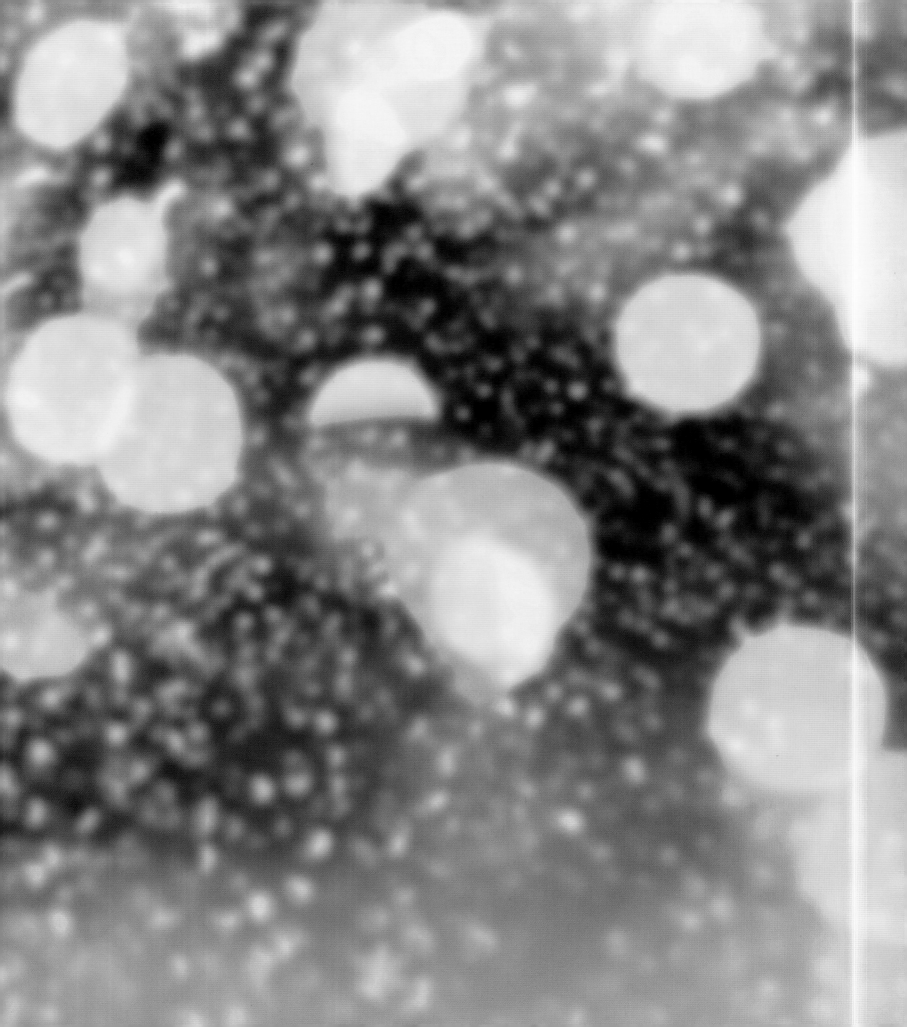

INDEX

CREDITS

PICTURE CREDITS

The publishers would like to thank the following sources for their kind permission to reproduce the pictures in this book. The page numbers for each of the photographs are listed below, giving the page on which they appear in the book.

AKG Images: 42R; /A Dagli Orti/De Agostini Picture Library: 36L; /Jean Tholance/Les Arts Decoratifs, Paris: 81
The Advertising Archives: 103T, 105TR
Alamy: /Archivart: 140L, 140R; /allOver images: 60–61; /Bon Appetit: 89BR, 117BL; /Paul Collins: 75TL; /DGDImages: 134T; /Iaroslav Danylchenko: 8-9; /Jean-Pierre Degas/Hemis: 52; /Julian Eales: 111BL; /f8 archive: 138TR; /Tim Graham: 111L; /Robert Harding: 46R, 110TR; /Hemis: 116TR; /Per Karlsson/BKWine.com: 116BR; /John Kellerman: 47B; /David Levenson: 73TR; /Lordprice Collection: 23T, 77, 89BL, 115TR; /Martin Norris Travel Photography: 98; /Mary Evans Picture Library: 83TR; /Nobel Images: 58L; /North Wind Picture Archives: 35B; /Prixpics: 68T; /Teofil Rewers: 131TR; /Bertrand Rieger/Hemis: 26; /Olivier Roux/Sagaphoto.com: 59B, 68B, 102TR; /Richard Soberka/Hemis: 107
Bibliotheque Nationale de France: 45L
Champagne Billecart-Salmon: 54TR, 54BL, 54BR, 55T, 55B
Bridgeman Images: /Gerald Bloncourt: 46L; /Look and Learn/Barbara Loe Collection: 71T; /PVDE: 83TR; /The Stapleton Collection: 13T, 13B, 15R, 78BL, 80T
Champagnes & Châteaux Canard Duchêne: 108BR
Leif Carlsson/Magazine

Vigneron: 94BL
Cephas: /Tom Hyland: 116BL; /Mick Rock: 3, 17B, 19B, 25T, 71B, 117TR
Getty Images: /Sergi Alexander: 106; /Andia/UIG: 8; /Ann Ronan Pictures/The Print Collector: 32L; /Apic: 43; /Art Media/The Print Collector: 36R; /BSIP/UIG: 19T; /Robyn Beck/AFP: 88BL; /Benainous/Vandeville/Gamma-Rapho: 75BL; /David M Benett: 24R; /Bettmann: 44L, 139T, 145T; /Walter Bibikow/age fotostock: 15L; /Michael Busselle/The Image Bank: 112–113; /Buyenlarge: 31BR; /Anne-Laure Camilleri/Gamma-Rapho: 21B; /Julia Claxton/Barcroft Media: 132–133; /Carl Court: 135T; /G Dagli Orti/De Agostini: 31TR; /Mark Downey Lucid Images/Corbis: 143; /Bruno Ehrs: 104; /Pepe Franco: 125T; /Owen Franken: 117BR; /David Goddard: 134B; /Brian Hagiwara/The LIFE Images Collection: 139B; /Andrew Harrer/Bloomberg: 22; /Hendrik Holler/StockFood Creative: 20R; /Hulton Archive: 31L; /Ady Kerry/Bloomberg: 135B; /Alexis Komenda: 50L; /Peter Macdiarmid: 131B; /Alastair Miller/Bloomberg: 20BL; /Jonathan Nackstrand/AFP: 152; /Francois Nascimbeni/AFP: 28R, 105BL, 109TR, 109B, 110BR; /Charles O'Rear/Corbis/VCG: 74; /PHAS/UIG: 29T; /Popperfoto: 145BL; /The Print Collector: 32R; /Bertrand Rieger/Hemis: 148TL; /Peter Richardson/Robert Harding: 148R; /Maurice Rougemont/Gamma-Rapho: 69T; /Ilya S Savenok: 123L; /Science & Society Picture Library: 138BR; /Lucas Schifres/Bloomberg: 47T; /Emmanuele Scorcelletti/Paris Match: 76, 130; /Barbara

Singer/Hulton Archive: 40; /Paul Slade/Paris Match: 88BR; /Kristy Sparrow: 115B; /Oliver Strewe/Lonely Planet Images: 149; /Pierre Suu: 6–7; /Warner Brothers: 144
Champagne Gosset: 62L, 62R, 63T, 63BR; /©Leif Carlsson: 63BL
iStockphoto: 12
Jacquart & Associés Distribution: 5, 115TL
Champagne Jacquesson: 66L, 66R, 67T, 67B
Champagne Joseph Perrier: 69B
Champagne Lanson: 51L, 72T, 72B, 73TL, 73B
Laurent-Perrier: 75BR
Library of Birmingham: 142
Limm Communications Ltd.: 64L, 64R, 65T, 65B
Champagne Mailly Grand Cru: /©Alain Proust: 114
Maisons Marques et Domaines: 18L, 18R, 25B, 94TR, 94BR, 95T, 95B, 96–97, 96B, 97R, 153
The Map House: 29B
Mary Evans Picture Library: 56TR; /Grenville Collins Postcard Collection: 45R; /Musee Carnavalet/Roger-Violett: 35T; /The Roseries Collection: 28L, 34; /Sammlung Rauch/Interfoto: 105BR
Mentzendorff & Co.: 51R, 56L, 56BR, 57T, 57B, 110BL, 147
Moët Hennessy: 33BR, 33TR, 37, 38-39, 58R, 59T, 70TR, 70BL, 99T, 99B, 101, 108TR, 108BL, 136; /©Andreas Achmann: 78BR, 79B; /©Thierry Desouches: 70BR; /© Moët & Chandon: 79T
G.H. Mumm: 21T, 82TR, 82BL, 82BR, 83B
PA Images: /AP: 90B; /Andrew Matthews: 131TL
Perrier-Jouët: 84TR, 84BL, 84BR, 85T, 85B

Champagne Philipponnat: 16, 23B, 50R, 86T, 86B, 87B; /Leif Carlsson: 87T
Pol Roger: 20BC, 90T, 91T, 91BL, 91BR
Private Collection: 41
Réunion des Musées Nationaux: Martine Beck-Coppola: 37BC; Le Studio Numérique: 37BL, 37BR.
Champagne Salon Delamotte: /©Serge Chapuis: 111BR
Christian Schopphoven: 80B
Shutterstock: 14, 33L, 111T, 120R, 141TR, 141BR; /joan_bautista: 118, 124; /Natalia Bratslavsky: 48–49; /Danita Delmont: 126TL; /Everett Collection/REX: 146; /FiledIMAGE: 127B; /T Furthmayr/REX: 123R; /gg-foto: 128–129; /Daan Kloeg: 150–151; /lusia83: 121; /magicbeam: 126B; /Sergey Mironov: 160; /Danny Moloshok/Invision/AP/REX: 126TR; /Melinda Nagy: 154-155; /Alessia Pierdomenico: 122; /Luz Rosa: 127T; /Warner Brothers/Everett Collection/REX: 145BR /ZRyzner: 125B
Champagne Taittinger: 17T, 102BL, 102BR; /©Michel Jolyot: 103B
Topfoto: 44R; /ullsteinbild: 109TL
Vranken-Pommery Monopole: 89T, 92TR, 92BL, 92BR, 93TL, 93TR, 93C, 93B, 148BL
Wikimedia Commons: 30L, 30R, 42L, 78TR, 88TR, 100, 120L, 138BL, 141BL

Every effort has been made to acknowledge correctly and contact the source and/or copyright holder of each picture and Carlton Books Limited apologises for any unintentional errors or omissions that will be corrected in future editions of this book.

FURTHER READING

• *The Champagne Companion* – Michael Edwards
• *Champagne – A Global History* – Becky Sue Epstein
• *The Champagne Guide* – Tyson Stelzer
• *Champagne: How the World's Most Glamorous Wine Triumphed Over War and Hard Times* – Don & Petie Kladstrup
• *Christie's World Encyclopedia of Champagne & Sparkling Wine* – Tom Stevenson, Essi Avellan
• *Destination Champagne* – Philippe Boucheron
• *No More Champagne: Churchill and his Money* – David Lough
• *The Story of Champagne* – Nicholas Faith
• *When Champagne Became French* – Kolleen Guy